I've Got the Blues: Looking for Justice in a Red State

by

Sharon Edge Martin

ISBN: 978-1-936923-34-2

First Edition March 2020

Cover Art by Dale Martin

Village Books Press
Santa Fe, New Mexico

Justice for some isn't justice at all.

This book is dedicated to
all those who have been denied justice or due process
for any reason in this country,
and
to the social justice warriors who keep trying to fulfill
this country's promise
of justice for all.

TABLE OF CONTENTS

INTRODUCTION

It's rare when a single voice can pierce the cacophony of the town square for more than a historical split second. It's even rarer when that voice becomes transcendent, an enduring source of wisdom and inspiration for generations.

Will Rogers had that gift. So did Woody Guthrie. Through humor and song, they laid bare the human condition from the absurd to the sublime. They spoke truth to power. And they helped point us to our better angels.

In early 21st century Oklahoma, Sharon Martin serves as that voice.

Writer, teacher, prophet, Sharon brings clarity to a world that often seems to be spinning out of control a world rife with overt racism and religious bigotry, hyper political partisanship and mounting income inequality, social media vitriol and sharply divided families.

This collection of essays, many of which first appeared in The Oklahoma Observer, speaks to, and helps make sense of, the issues of a specific era. But really, it's timeless.

Though the generations change, the issues largely remain the same. Sharon's insightful prose no doubt will apply then, as now.

As a public school instructor and reading specialist, it's hardly surprising Sharon focused much of her decade-plus essay writing on education policy and its impact on students, teachers, communities and Oklahoma's future. But she also fearlessly weighed in on some of society's most ferocious debates from patriarchy and immigration to healthcare and worker rights.

What makes Sharon's prose especially powerful is that she deploys a scalpel, not a sledgehammer in seeking to enlighten and inform. Myriad studies suggest lecturing, browbeating, often has the opposite effect: it doesn't change another's point of view, it hardens it.

Sharon's essays offer food for thought. Plainly worded, yet elegant. Full of common sense. Laser focused on what's really at issue, and what's really at stake. And, yes, she can rabble rouse, if necessary!

As you read and ponder this collection, it will become evident why Sharon's Observer essays are among the most shared on social media. She is an Oklahoma treasure whose clear-eyed takes on the day's challenges are destined to long be remembered.

Arnold Hamilton, Editor
The Oklahoma Observer
August 2019

What Teachers Know: One Teacher's List

Some smart kids don't test well.

What helps a kid score well on the next test isn't necessarily what makes him a thinker or a lifelong learner.

There are no quick fixes.

Not everyone will arrive at the benchmarks set by researchers and legislators at the same time. Some never reach them.

When a student learns to think for herself, she will have the tools she needs to educate herself. This, not a head full of random facts, should be the goal of educators.

Size matters. In small schools, where teachers know every child's name…and their parents and their grandparents…fewer kids fall through the cracks.

Class size matters even more. Research proves that 14 to 18 students in a classroom give the best results.

Too many legislators ignore good education research.

Parents are the single most important component in a child's education. If parents are involved in a meaningful way—teaching what they know, reading to and with their child, having real conversations with them about real topics—the student is much more likely to be a success.

Public schools are not, as a self-described Tea Party member once said, indoctrination machines. They can be, however, scary places if your eight-year-old is afraid he'll flunk third-grade year because he doesn't read as well as his friends.

National standards are not the enemy.

Standards that ignore development psychology are. It is futile to push students to learn a subject before their minds are ready.

Recess matters. So do lunch breaks and cooperative learning opportunities. Social skills are an essential part of the informal curriculum.

Hands-on activities beat workbooks almost every time. It is experiences and not worksheets that students will remember.

Music, art, and life skills should be part of every curriculum.

We do not have too many administrators. The work that superintendents and principals do make possible the work that teachers do. Ask any veteran teacher about the importance of a good administrator.

Education doesn't end at the schoolhouse door or on graduation day. It lasts a lifetime.

Sending young people into the world with a passion for knowledge and for the work they have chosen are our goals. This, not earning power, test scores, or Ivy League degrees, should be how we measure education success.

September 2015

Civility and Common Ground

The Democratic debate was civil. The candidates discussed ideas and solutions. Why are we surprised? When did presidential elections become a media affair? When did it become socially acceptable to be an ass?

Candidates have always found less than polite ways to draw distinctions between themselves. Remember the Hamilton/Burr duel? But in the past few years, things have gotten mighty ugly.

If you want the U.S. to be respected again, here are some things to consider: It is okay to be friends with people outside your political party.

People of different religions are not your enemy. Equal rights and equal protection under the law are not persecution of those who practice the dominant religion.

Humans are on a continuum between extremes. On one end are those who are afraid of anyone who doesn't look like them, think like them, believe as they do. On the other end are the folk who would draw no boundaries, welcome in everyone, share all resources. Most of us approach the center.

If you base your political affiliation on a single issue, you will vote against your self-interest. We have to pick the candidate who most closely aligns with our beliefs on a variety of issues.

You can probably find something on which you and any other person, including presidential candidates from both parties, can agree. Find that common ground.

No one should fear social justice. If we deny it to others, there's a chance that we will lose it for ourselves.

Diversity, in ideas and in the gene pool, makes the human race stronger.

Neither socialism nor capitalism is a dirty word. The sweet spot is somewhere between the two systems.

What should our elected representatives do? How about they work for the people they represent instead of for their parties. How about they work together.

Not only is all or nothing unfair, it is dangerous. Compromise isn't about abandoning ones ideals but about finding workable solutions.

Diplomacy trumps war. It is not our place to overthrow the dictators in other countries, especially given the rise of fascism in our own.

Civility can make working together easier. Together we can stop the would-be warlords who would destroy our democracy. Where do we start?

Quit the name calling and hateful rhetoric.
Practice kindness.
Have hard conversations.
Seek understanding.
Ignore the asses and ignoramuses, and don't be either of those things yourself.

When you vote, consider not only your own best interest but also that of your fellow citizens.

Be politically active. Politics affect you personally.

Vote!

This will do for a start.

October 2015

Feed My Children

In a free and wealthy country, there should be no pockets of hunger.

In an age of enlightenment, food should provide nourishment, not just taste and calories.

And if we want to survive as modern humans, we should be prepared for whatever the natural world and international politics throws at us.

We shouldn't be dependent on corporations for our daily bread, and we should be prepared if a climate catastrophe occurs. Local food is essential to homeland security.

During World War II, folks at home aided the war effort by raising chickens and growing gardens. This let food manufacturers concentrate on feeding our troops around the world.

There was a reservoir of knowledge about food production and preparation. Cooks may not have had their choice of a dozen cooking shows, but they had mothers, social clubs, and neighbors who taught them what they needed to know.

Every food had a season. Homemakers put away strawberries in spring and dug potatoes in early summer. They canned peaches, tomatoes, and green beans when they came ripe. Fall was for applesauce and cider, for sweet potatoes and winter squashes that would last the winter.
A core of citizens interested in the local economy and whole foods are bringing back some of these skills. Families are gardening with their children. Cooks are filling family pantries. But we need to do more to be sure that everyone is included in this food revolution.

Weather is unpredictable, but climate has patterns. The average date for the last spring freeze in my area is mid-April. Two of the last three years have seen no freeze past mid-March. These two warm springs and mild summers were separated by a May snow and early fall frost. As a long-time gardener, I see the swings of unpredictably getting wilder.

Now, past the average date for the first fall frost in my zone, I'm keeping an eye on tomato plants loaded with fruit and think that, in these unpredictable times, when commercial agriculture depends on patterns and abundant resources, we need to make sure we have safeguards in place. Every person needs to know how to feed himself.

If schools are to really address the needs of learners, gardening, hunter safety, conservation, and nutrition should be part of the school curriculum.

As the climate changes, education may save our country as surely as the victory gardens, backyard chickens, and common knowledge helped save the world in the 1940s.

We must start now.

November 2015

Ripped Off and Damned Mad

We Americans work our tails off, and for what? There is always a line of someones—insurance companies, phone companies, the cable company, oil companies, and the bankers who get a penny or two off every transaction—who have figured out how to take what we've earned.

Then there are the politicians who work for these someones. Their job is to make us angry at anyone in the government who wants to make sure we have a little bit of something left when we turn 65, access to low-cost healthcare, affordable birth control, education, clean air, drinkable water, opportunities.

Yes, Americans are angry. And we are misled. Too many politicians and television personalities owe their jobs to our fear and anger.

In case you didn't know it, there's an election coming. Some of the candidates would just as soon you didn't care. That's how they get elected. But you must pay attention to politics, because it affects you whether you're listening or not.

Prepare to vote. Don't take anyone's advice but your own, and do your research before you go to the polls. Don't settle for one source of information on anything, even if you want to believe it.

We are the government, at least for the time being. So speak up. Our voices, our votes, and the few dollars we have left are our best weapons against the real enemies of democracy, unregulated commerce and manufactured fear.

December 2015

What Is It Good For?

Marauding Buddhist monks terrorize citizens in Myanmar. Buddhists, for heaven's sake! An avowed Christian kills three at a Planned Parenthood clinic. Two Christian patriots blow up the federal building in Oklahoma City. Hindus and Muslims clash. Israelis and Palestinians deny each other their humanity and common ancestry. Men who have subverted Islam kill followers of their own prophet. It is hard to believe that every one of these religions has some form of the golden rule in its sacred text.

What makes some true believers work for peace while others strap on the vest? Why do followers of Trump and Cruz and most of the GOP lineup glorify war? Is it DNA or personal choice that determines our path?

Whichever it is, the last Republican debate was a shout-out to our baser instincts. We know we're in trouble when Rand Paul, who espouses Ayn Rand's philosophy of selfishness, is the voice of reason.

Maybe we see and hear too much. Videos, photographs, talk shows, and one-liners stir us up. Pundits and politicians know what they're doing. They prefer passions to logic.

Stalin knew how easy it was to sway the masses. "You only have to make them believe they are under attack," he said.

One attack leads to another, tit for tat. Extended wars brought down the Roman Empire. It can bring down our mighty nation. War brings great profit to a few, but there is nothing left for the average citizen or even the returning warriors when all the bills are paid.

War does not bring peace. Didn't World War I, World War II, the Korean War, the Vietnam War, and every war after not teach us anything?

War does not save lives. What are the lives of four thousand American soldiers worth? What about the hundred thousand Iraqis, both civilian and military? We killed more Iraqis than Saddam ever did. Is there any question why the survivors are angry? We destabilized a secular country and set the current troubles into motion. Now we must deal with the rebels we created and armed. Denigrating all Muslims for the actions of the extremists isn't the answer. Neither is ignoring the plight of the refugees who are running from the extremists.

During this season of peace, I pray we say no to the fear mongers and the haters. As historian Howard Zinn said, "How can you have a war on terrorism when war itself is terrorism?"

December 2015

Dismantling Public Education

If your idea of good governance is to take care of the top ten percent of the citizens in your state, your first job will be to take down public education.

In the first minutes of Mary Fallin's 2016 State of the State Address, she called her policy-induced budget disaster "an economic crisis that is largely out of our control." But don't worry. "We can use this budget crisis to build a solid foundation for Oklahoma with meaningful fiscal reform that the state needs."

This makes sense if by "out of our control" she is acknowledging that someone outside her office and the legislature were behind the tax cuts and credits that gutted the treasury. Now, what does she mean by fiscal reform?

One of her ideas for replacing revenue lost to tax cuts is a use tax on previously exempted services. What services does she have in mind? Medical services? Automotive services? While the wealthiest Oklahomans pay less income tax, the rest of us will take up the slack if our heater goes out or our roof needs fixing?

She warned school administrators of mid-year cuts but wants to give teachers a raise.

Education cuts and teacher raises might make sense if you add consolidation. In our school, there are teachers with as many as 30 students. Research tells us that a class size of 14 to 18 students gives the best results. But if you double class size and give half as many teachers a $3,000 raise, you've saved money. Brilliant!

Since we've already dug ourselves a budget hole, let's dig a little deeper with Education Savings Accounts. The governor proposes to take per-pupil funds from public schools and give them to parents who send their kids to private schools. There goes that raise.

Let's sum it up: we have a financial crisis because we cut income taxes and we have a glut of oil that affects the value of one of our main commodities in Oklahoma. We like our tax cuts, so we're going to raise taxes on the poor and middle class to keep them.

Our schools are starving for money, so we're going to consolidate. That won't save us any money, according to policy makers who have studied this, but we've already seen class size increase. To save even more, we're going to give part of our money to private schools where there is no accountability. And we're going to give teachers a raise.

There. You have what passes for critical thinking in Oklahoma politics where public education is considered the enemy.

February 2016

What Privatize Really Means

You want to sell our public lands
and pristine places,

turn public service
into for-profit business

until everything is owned
by a handful of old men

with nothing invested
and nothing to lose,

paid for by the sweat of the rest of us,
those to whom this land belongs.

We already stole it
fair and square,

with our guns and plows
and relentless westward movement
from the natives whose ancient clans
called themselves the people. First people.

You want the blacks to be subservient,
women to be chattel again,
Indians to disappear.

Something went wrong
in that first attempt to erase them.
Something went wrong
in the centuries of owning, silencing,
burning and hanging the wise ones.
Something went wrong
when one of them squatted
in the White House.

No way he can be legit
when a handful of rich folk,
enriched and empowered to govern
by a smaller handful of even richer folk,
didn't give him permission
to be the most powerful man
in the world.

You want your place of privilege sealed
by cutting wages,
cutting services,

leaving us the jobs
of staying in the shadows,
keeping quiet,
paying the taxes,
dying on the battlefields,

laboring for your gain,
in this plutocracy
that you've convinced too many voters
is their American Dream, too.

February 2016

It's the Economy, Stupid!

Racism runs roughshod over this year's primaries. Unrest, hate, and the absence of truth mark most candidacies. There's a real chance of boots-on-the-ground war if certain candidates make it to the White House.

What might be causing all this fear and loathing? Might it be the economy that serves too few of our citizens?

I'm an old woman and I've learned a few things over the years. What I'm about to say to you I didn't get from a blog or newspaper or television show, liberal or otherwise. These facts are the outcome of personal experience.

1. The stock market performs better during Democratic administrations.

2. Artists, sign painters, and other bellwethers of the wellbeing of the middle class make more money during Democratic administrations.

3. When the stock market tanks, those with billions hang on and wait for the rebound. But they aren't just waiting; they are buying the cheap stocks that the not-so-wealthy and not-so-savvy investors dump in the down times.

4. The mortgage crisis hurt the middle class. The wealthy could buy up houses in the depressed market to resell for a profit; the poor and middle class lost their homes and what savings they had in their homes.

5. Those who sold or repackaged the subprime loans legally robbed homeowners and investors.

6. What's good for the wealthy is seldom good for the middle class and the poor.

7. Too many poor and middle-class neighbors vote for candidates who mean them no good.

8. When the policies of these no-goodniks threaten the economy of those who vote for them, they trot out the propaganda that shifts the blame to workers, immigrants, the other party, anyone but those responsible.

9. The people who don't understand the way this rigged system works likely won't be reading this.

10. Those who are hurt the most by the self-serving politicians will believe the candidates who offer the most outlandish solutions to

their problems [like building a wall so white people can have those desirable migrant farmworker jobs].

11. Until we get big money out of politics, nothing will change.

12. Until Congress addresses *Citizens United*, nothing will change.

13. Until workers unionize and let big employers know that their wealth depends on them, nothing will change.

14. Until journalism is free of corporate restraints, nothing will change.

15. It's time to demand change.

March 2016

We Serve

Waiting outside the door of a classroom to pick up students for Reading Lab, I saw a second grader pointing at me.

"I know you," he said. "You're the table-washing lady."

I'm a reading specialist, but every teacher knows that teaching subject matter is only part of the job.

At our school we move 450 students through the cafeteria during lunch hour. This requires a system and a couple of busy table-washing ladies. As I wash tables between waves, the principals are mopping up spills and dispensing condiments at the salad bar. The speech pathologist is handing out milk cartons.

And this week, in addition to teaching students to read, do math, and wash their hands when they come out of the restroom, we are also overseeing a huge drain on the state's education budget, standardized testing.

Parents and lay staff have been enlisted. No teacher is ever alone in the classroom during testing. Nothing is allowed on students' desks but pencils, the test booklet, and the answer sheet. We have Quiet signs in the hallways. Phones and bells are silenced. And learning comes to a dead halt. I look forward to lunchroom duty.

How many legislators know what actually goes on in an elementary school? Do they know how many hugs are dispensed, like the medicine they are, every day? That kid with the lice? He's probably the first to ask for a hug.

How many legislators know how to check a kid's head for lice? Would our governor be willing to clean tables an hour every day? Who among the leaders would do these necessary jobs gladly?

I like lunchroom duty. It's where I really get to know the students, in their array of colorful personalities. I recognize the future scientists, the artists, and the bullies.

> Even here, teaching goes on.
> Don't shove.
> Watch out for your neighbor.
> Pick up your mess.

When my duty is over, I grab a tray and gobble down lunch in the teachers' lounge. Then I go back to the classroom to do what I was trained to do, teach kids to be critical thinkers when confronted with written and spoken words.

I love my job. But a cup of coffee or a bathroom break would be nice. So would a secure source of funding so no teacher has more students than she can see to. And we'd all like a little respect for all the jobs we do, including table washing.

April 2016

Robbing the Poor

Ever hear something that just stops you dead?

On NPR, Mara Liasson was discussing political polls. She said that Republicans don't poll well on women's issues.

That's easy to explain—unequal pay, attempts to control women's bodies, and family issues.

Then she said, "Republicans consistently outpoll Democrats on the economy."

Doesn't anyone remember the mess that Bush/Cheney left us? Or Reagan's deficit?

How about Senator Cruz's tantrum when it came time for America to pay her debts?

Then there's the funding mess in Oklahoma. When times were good, Fallin and Company gave huge breaks to the oil and gas producers and cut taxes on the wealthy. They cut services for the rest of us.

Their policies threaten schools, nursing homes, rural hospitals, and at-risk children. Prisons are for profit and understaffed. Still, they refuse federal money to insure the chronically uninsured. They eliminate programs that offer matching federal funds.

Oklahomans pay federal income taxes in return for federal programs, but Republicans would rather raise sales taxes that place the burden on the poor. They can't pass a budget bill that isn't toxic to the state on the one hand and to their re-election bids on the other.

There's more.

Speaker of the House, Jeff Hickman, sent a bill to the Senate that gives teachers a raise. But wait! He wants teachers and the school districts...yeah, those districts laying off employees and mulling four-day weeks...to pay for teacher insurance.

My insurance, according to Speaker Hickman, costs the state $6,360 a year. My salary, including insurance, is more than $10,000 below the median income in Oklahoma. I have a Master's degree. And you can bet if the state isn't paying for it, my insurance will cost me more than it does them.

Your proposal stinks, Speaker Hickman.

And still, there are teachers who vote Republican.

If that isn't enough, there's the Trump debacle. He's never been elected to an office in his life. He has run a few businesses, but he's filed for Chapter 11 bankruptcy at least four times.

Do you know what Chapter 11 does? It leaves a business's creditors holding the bag while protecting owners from personal liability.

Yep, that's the same idea that Senator Cruz was promoting with his filibuster. If you run out of money, just don't pay your bills. Unless you're poor and can't pay court costs. Then we'll throw you in jail.

Republicans are Reverse Robin Hoods. They take from the poor and give to the rich. And we keep voting for the Sheriff of Nottingham.

May 2016

Spin Machine

Listening to the Chairman of the Republican Party a couple of Sundays ago, two things were clear:

1. Power is more important to the Republicans than policy or people.
2. The GOP holds the Clintons to standards that they reject for themselves.

In one sentence Reince Priebus said that we shouldn't be bringing up old news about his candidate when what we should be talking about is what happened at Benghazi.

That's right, Chairman Priebus. Divert our attention from the warlord who wants to make this country great again for white men.

New voters are flocking to the polls. They say they are sick of the lying and the spin. But they buy into the spin. And they believe the lies.

A relative explained to me why he couldn't vote for Hillary.

"She was fired from the Watergate investigation for ethics violations."

When I pointed out that Snopes labeled this false, and suggested that Mr. Zeifman must be lying, especially since he was in no position to fire Ms. Rodham, he had an answer.

"Oh, it's everyone else who's lying about poor Hillary."

That's exactly what I was saying.

Here's the deal: the truth is the truth even if you don't want to believe it.

There are problems with the two-party system. Some people can't vote in the primaries. Some people's votes are worth more. The wealthy can buy power. There is room for new voices and new ideas. But for now, there is only one party who looks after the poor and middle class. Hint: it isn't the one whose candidate made it "on his own with only a small loan of a million dollars from his dad."

Inherited wealth doesn't disqualify him. No, it's his complete disregard for anyone's opinion but his own, his lack of impulse control, and his belief that his mistakes don't matter.

If he's president, they will matter a lot. We will be the ones who pay for them.

Our mistake will be listening to the spin and believing the lies. The mother of all mistakes would be to elect Donald Trump as president.

May 2016

One Issue Voters

Say you are pro-life. You want to stop abortions, but you don't want sex education. You don't want your taxes paying for birth control. You want to close the Planned Parenthood in your town, the only source of health care for some women and a fighter against the spread of STDs. Think about that for a while.

You're pro-unregulated Second Amendment, never mind what the Constitution says. You've never broken a law in your life, but you don't want to have to pass a background check because it infringes on your rights. How about the right to safe schools? The answer isn't more guns. If that were the case, the United States would be the safest country on earth.

You want to do something about the ravages of drugs and drug addiction on our culture. Good. That means you want to see drug courts and treatment programs expanded and affordable. And you want access to mental health care for everyone. Who pays for it?

You want cuts on income taxes? That benefits the wealthy. When revenues fail because of income tax loopholes, political favors, and other giveaways, they'll have to nickel and dime the rest of us with fees and sales tax increases.

What if I told you that an increase in income tax, especially on large incomes, would equate to a higher standard of living for the average person in the state? What if I told you that the states that spend the most money on education have the highest per capita income?

How about religious freedom? Is that your issue? Do you believe that religious freedom extends to all religions or just yours? Which religion? If you want a Christian theocracy, will it be Protestant or Catholic? Baptist or Lutheran? Who gets to decide what you have to believe?

The issues overlap in ways we can see and in ways that we can't. The thing is, we are all better off when there are no hunger zones, no pockets of hopelessness, no groups underemployed because of a lack of education.

Ask any candidate one question: do you think the promises of the Constitution and the opportunities of a Democratic Republic should be accessible to every citizen? If they can't properly answer that, start asking about single issues. Chances are, they won't have good answers about those, either.

Finally, ask them who is funding their run for office. That's where you'll find their priorities. Funding! That may be the single issue we should all be voting on.

June 2016

A Call for Honest News

If you believe a lie, you can probably find a website or news source that will back you up. If you want the truth, you must work for it. And you must think about it.

If you browse Facebook, you may have seen the picture of Laura Bush with the heading that called her a Hillary Clinton supporter. How many people read the article behind the heading? The former First Lady never said she supported Secretary Clinton. What she made clear was that she didn't support Trump.

A real journalist doesn't make up misleading headlines...even if they think it will please their readers!

There are news sources that I don't even bother to read any more, despite the fact that I support the same causes they do. The headlines aren't accurate. They use politically charged words when the facts are all we need.

Good investigative journalism, politically relevant or not, lays out the facts and lets you make your own connections. Think critically.

For example, did you see the piece about Saudi Arabia on *Frontline*? Did you make the connection between the Saudi Religious Police who brutally enforce their own personal brand of Sharia Law and your Muslim-hating uncle who wants our laws to enforce Old Testament justice?

Your uncle votes, and if he's like mine, he votes for the guy who calls himself a law and order conservative. Find out what that means. If you don't, these self-styled Christian patriots can turn the U.S. into a Christian version of Saudi Arabia.

Your uncle searches online for opinion pieces and outright lies to support his personal beliefs. He then passes them on. If you try to argue with him, his lies become a thread on your Facebook page.

Don't argue.

Search for the truth, but before you spread it, make sure it is the whole truth.

Know your biases.

Use common sense and commonsense tools like PolitiFact and Snopes.

There are benefits of sticking to the truth and avoiding politically charged language. One is that you may be able to find common ground with folks on the other side of the political divide and have a real conversation.

July 2016

Fixing What's Broken

There are a lot of angry people in our country. Anger is one of the drivers in this year's presidential election. Anger and fear. At the end of the cavalcade, I see hope. He's way back there.

No matter who wins…and believe me, it matters…the anger will still be there. So will the fear. So what do we do to bring the people in this country together? There are plenty of things we need to fix—campaign finance laws; inequality in the education and justice systems; and access to quality, affordable healthcare, for starters. This is what this old social justice liberal sees as the most pressing issues, but I'm one of the privileged. I have a job, a home, a car. I have health insurance.

Poverty and income inequality cause issues that some of us can't even imagine to come to the forefront. The people who need advocates in government are often those so overwhelmed with problems that voting isn't even on their radar. They get what they don't vote for, and they're often angry at the wrong people.

Political activists on the other side of the aisle are worried about national security. It's a social science fact that conservatives are the gatekeepers against intruders and liberals are the gate openers to new ideas. It has always been so, and the safety and advancement of the human race requires a balance between the two sides.

History, too, tells us that balance works to the benefit of the citizens. When Democrats and Republicans (or whatever parties come to power in the next century) work together, the people win. When CEOs make

money, but not too much, and their workers make enough money to support their families, the people win. Balance.

So, how do we come together at the center? Can we start with common ground? Right now, the common ground is hard to find. But the future of this nation depends on us finding it. Perhaps it starts with respectful conversation.

Let's talk. Let's listen. Let's try to understand each other's positions. Let's do it now, before it's too late.

August 2016

Why Words Matter

Kids with a healthy vocabulary score better on tests. They make better grades. They make a good impression in interviews. They aren't necessarily smarter than other kids, but they have any easier time getting through school.

As a reading teacher, I see this bear out day after day and year after year. Vocabulary matters. And something else I know: kids don't learn vocabulary by filling in worksheets.

Vocabulary building begins at birth. Some say it begins before that, with the sound of a mother's voice. It is built around the dinner table and in Mama's lap. It is built in churches, theaters, museums, and in all the interactions children have with adults. It is impossible to underestimate the benefits of books, conversation, and social interaction during a child's early years.

A group of researchers, led by Mariah Evans, University of Nevada, Reno, found in a 20-year study that books in the home have an effect on the education level a child will attain equal. Having 500 books in the home will add an average of 3.2 years to a child's education. Low-income children benefit most.

Two groups seek to get books into the hands of low-income children—First Book and Reading Is Fundamental. My Title 1 program is fortunate to be a beneficiary of First Book. You should see how excited students get when boxes of books arrive!

Last spring, as the school year was coming to a close, third and fourth graders left the classroom clutching a book of poetry to their chests. We received hardback copies of Caroline Kennedy's *A Family of Poems.* We read poems aloud in class, as a chorus, to each other, sometimes with drum accompaniment.

"Someday, you'll read these poems to your children," I said. I was thinking of my Grandma Edge who shared poems with me.

We start where we are and try to have an impact on this generation and the next.

Louis Foley understood the importance of words. In his 1928 book, *Beneath the Crust of Words*, he wrote this: "Knowing words, realizing what they are, and understanding something of how they have come to be what they are, we see in them the crystallized residue of many centuries of thought."

If we want children to grow up to be thinkers, we have to give them the words that give flesh to their ideas. We have to talk to them about things of importance. We have to share stories with them and put books into their hands.

Civilization depends on us to get this job done.

August 2016

Let's Stand Together!

When I first started teaching, I paid all but a few dollars of my insurance premium. It didn't seem fair that legislators got family coverage, paid for by taxpayers, when teachers did not even get personal coverage paid.

Thankfully, the Oklahoma Education Association rallied members and fought for our insurance coverage. Even those teachers who didn't belong to the union benefitted.

Unions are good for workers. Unions set the standards, for wages and conditions. Think about the forty-hour week, overtime pay, and safety rules that we take for granted in this country and that we are in danger of losing.

A friend went to work for a local firm some years ago. The company managed several warehouses, and when a new warehouse went online, it was necessary for employees to work weekends. In return, the company gave salaried employees comp time.

When a corporation whose name everyone recognizes bought the company, things began to change. Recently, they gave my friend a one-day notice that she would be working both Saturday and Sunday. She has small children and a husband whose days off aren't on weekends. She hadn't scheduled a babysitter.

When she asked about comp time, she was told that they "didn't have to give comp time." They also told her to expect a lot of working weekends.

With a graduate degree, my friend could have earned more at another job, but she stayed because the company took care of her. That seems to have changed. Too bad she and her fellow employees aren't union members.

Business has always been about the bottom line. But someone seems to have forgotten the value of a contented and loyal workforce.

There are employers who value the workers who earn money for them. There are also those who want something for as close to nothing as they can get.

These employers would rather pay a politician than an employee. They rally against immigration reform and hire illegals because they can get away with paying them less. They bought right to work laws with campaign contributions. They also gave you the Triangle Shirtwaist Fire, the Ludlow Massacre, and the Haymarket Riot. People died for our right to unionize.

It is no coincidence that wages have stagnated as union membership has fallen, that people are working longer hours for less. Unions protect your pension, your health, and the right to a decent living for a hard week's work.

It is time for Oklahoma workers to swell union ranks. That includes Oklahoma's underpaid teachers. Perhaps the legislature will take us more seriously if we take our rights as workers more seriously.

September 2016

Innocent Unless You Scare Me

When I took a conceal carry class, one of the things that stuck with me was the teacher's insistence that if I felt my life was in danger, I shouldn't hesitate to shoot.

What is a life worth? What is my life worth against someone else's? When is the right time for fear to make our decisions for us?

Sometimes we are caught between competing desires, one for safety and the other for justice. This is personal for me. I want my son-in-law, a police officer, to come home to his family, my family, at the end of each shift. I want every suspect with whom he has contact to be innocent until proven guilty.

We no longer abide gangs of white men lynching black men. Today, someone would have paid for the death of Emmett Till. I hope. But too many brown people and poor people and damaged people are still denied justice, some of them simply out of a police officer's fear.

Part of this has to be cultural bias.

Poet Sly Alley writes in "We Are All Woodcarvers," a tribute to First Nation's artist, John T. Williams, who was shot as he crossed the street in Seattle carrying a piece of cedar and his carving knife.

At an art show here in Oklahoma I saw a friend hauled away by the police because a woman reported that she had seen him on America's Most Wanted. A successful sculptor and potter, this artist is also a big black man with a head full of dreadlocks. He was forced to leave his booth and was taken downtown for questioning, suffering only fear and a loss of dignity. In a different city, on a different street, this, too, could have ended tragically.

We are innocent until proven guilty. Our Constitution is supposed to guarantee this. Even Dylann Roof, who shot nine people in a church in Charleston, who left a witness to his rampage, is assured due process.

Dylann Roof was taken alive to face justice.

So should Terence Crutcher have been.
If the law can't grant justice to Mr. Crutcher, it won't protect any of us. I grieve for his family.

I grieve for Officer Shelby's family. There are no winners here.

October 2016

Slanting the Polls

Teachers in Oklahoma were asked to take part in a political poll from SoonerPoll and the Oklahoman. SoonerPoll calls itself nonpartisan. The Oklahoman definitely is not. Despite my doubts, I decided to answer the questions.

> Was I registered to vote? Yes
> Did I intend to vote in the presidential election? Yes
> Who did I support? Hillary Clinton

Then came a question asking me which category of issues was most important to me. The first was Social Issues. Their definition included "marriage protection." Okay, so what's their definition of nonpartisan?

The second choice was Economic Issues. That definition included "lower spending" and "job creation." I thought of all the social workers and teachers who'd been laid off because of spending cuts and how the state's budget balancing act never required more money from those who can afford it, only cuts for those who can't.

The last two choices were Education and Other. The definition for Education included something about Charters. I didn't finish the poll. How could I? There was nothing about providing every child a good education. There was nothing about social justice. There was nothing about ensuring that every citizen in the state had access to healthcare. They didn't address corruption in the political system.

I wonder how many other progressive voters—people who believe in marriage equality, who believe that some government spending is necessary to insure equality of access and opportunity, who believe that a strong public school system is the foundation of our democracy—will finish this poll.

If the questions are slanted, how valid are the results?
Are there any polls that are truly nonpartisan?

With Russia hacking into voting records, polls asking seriously biased questions, and a demented man the choice of so many voters, I'm feeling woozy.

Someone, throw me a little hope.

October 2016

Real Economics

"Obamacare destroyed the economy of the United States," a friend of mine wrote.

Hospitals in Oklahoma shut down because we didn't accept the Medicaid expansion. That did indeed knock a hole in the economy of some small towns. But it wasn't the ACA that did it; it was Republicans playing M*ake Sure Obama Loses* that did the trick.

It started with Chief Justice Roberts' clever tactic to declare the ACA constitutional but let states opt out of key parts.

Listen, we pay for the uninsured, with higher premiums and lower productivity. Insuring 20 million more people didn't hurt the

economy. We'd be better off if everyone were covered. Did your candidate propose that?

Republican policies are not good for the poor and middle class. Why do so many hardworking people vote for bad economic policies? They're not voting for a Teddy Roosevelt to break up monopolies or a Dwight Eisenhower to promote the interstate highway system. They're voting for men and women who turn up their noses at constituents' needs.

Excuse me if I paint Republican lawmakers with a broad brush, but most of them seem to be in lockstep, marching against progress and economic prosperity for the people they supposedly serve.

Democrats need to be more assertive. We need to point out fallacies in so-called conservative arguments and show proof that our policies benefit hardworking men and woman.

Forget the propaganda. America can deal with social issues without bankrupting the middle class and starving the poor.

State taxes in Oklahoma have been cut and the people chiseled. Public schools are hungry. Prisons have become a corporate moneymaker. We hear calls for bringing in new industries even as the legislature turns the treasury over to oil and gas companies.

Now, the Trump administration seeks to follow the devastating example of Oklahoma and other red states.

Speaker Ryan's plan to *save* Social Security lets younger workers create their own retirement programs. Yep, we're all financial wizards now. You're not? Don't worry. A broker will take care of it for you. The only things you'll have to worry about are brokerage fees and market fluctuations.

Remember what happened to your 401k during the last downturn? What if that were your Social Security? Who does privatizing Social Security benefit? Hint: it's not retirees.

You can study competing theories of economics, but they are really competing moral theories. The GDP doesn't matter if all the earnings being generated go to a chosen few. Hunger and despair don't make us more secure.

Which theory gives economic security to the greatest number of people? Is that the one your candidates promise to follow?

November 2016

Freedom to Believe

It is not a character flaw to not be a Christian.

We find it hard to trust someone who doesn't believe what we believe. This is what makes religion...and politics...such dangerous subjects.

If you're a true believer, people who don't buy into your belief system are suspect. But religions rise up in particular places, based on the experiences of the people. If you have never seen a volcano, no way can you understand a deity like Pelée. Like the Fire Goddess, Jesus fulfills a need and calms our fears.

More than thirty percent of the world's people call themselves Christians. More than two-thirds do not.

Before the age of mass communication and global travel, sharing information was a long, hard journey. There were pockets of people who would never get your message. And if they didn't believe as you did...because the message had never reached them...what then? Were they doomed to hell by your God?

Religions are guidelines by which to live. If your guideline preaches hate, you're either reading the rules wrong or you need a different religion. Religious beliefs that don't make us better people have human problems.

We see it in groups like ISIS, for sure, but we also see it in Christians who banish nonbelievers, in marauding Buddhists, in Hindus fighting Muslims, in Puritans who hang women they call witches, in churches who believe people born gay deserve to die.

There are different routes to heaven, if heaven exists and whatever it's called. There are enough resources for us all if we share. And there's enough room for every belief that doesn't cause harm to other humans.

The U.S. Constitution guarantees us the right to worship, or not, as we choose. Why, then, does anyone believe it is constitutional...or American...to discriminate against Muslims?

I am ashamed of what happened in our country this week, of our president, and that we haven't welcomed more people fleeing the horrors of war.

I am proud of the people who stood up—civil servants, citizens, cab drivers, lawyers, everyone who acted, everyone who told the president that he was wrong.

Muslims are not bad people. Christians are not bad people. Neither are Jews, pagans, humanists, agnostics, Wiccans, or members of the 4,200 religions in the world. Okay, some of them are bad, but it isn't because of religion.

Slow down, Mr. President. Seek wise counsel. Make friends around the world so we can all work together to stop the few who would do us harm.

January 2017

Bring It On

Have you felt like curling into a ball and crying these last two weeks? The bald-faced cruelty of the Trump administration has left me heartsick.

People who had been through years-long screening were turned away from our door and sent back to nothing. They'd sold their personal property and quit jobs. Some left family waiting at the airline gate. Some were returned to certain danger.

And none of it makes us safer. Or richer, unless your portfolios are heavy with defense stocks.

Just two weeks in, and we are already tired. We're tired of marching, tired of responding to lies, tired of protesting the latest cruelty. This regime is counting on that. If they wear us out, they win.

If you find yourself faltering, an Oklahoma City poet has some suggestions. Jennifer E. Hudgens urges us not only to keep "speaking up and out against hate" and "being good humans" but also to "make art."

“I know some really amazing folks,” she adds.

So do I. And some of them voted for the president. The arrogance to think that only we have the answers will do no one any good. We need to listen as well as speak up, but we can’t be okay with lies and hate.

So, buck up. Get up each day armed with your best weapons—kindness and a determination to know the truth.

Fighting back is grueling work, but there are positives. Food isn’t being rationed…yet. We don’t need to carry identification papers to go to work…yet. We can still gather and speak and stand in the open.

And we have tools. Purpose, courage, books, and beauty can help us carry on. Time spent with friends and loved ones will keep us from getting burned out by the fight. A walk in the woods or neighborhood park does everyone some good.

Poets and musicians, keep writing and performing, and not just protest poems and fight songs. Writers, painters, and sculptors, keep creating. Art and beauty are not only necessary to our lives but to the fight. If it weren’t so, cuts to the National Endowment for the Arts and its sister organization wouldn’t have been among the first announced.

Soldiers aren’t the only ones who will fight to keep us free. Artists will keep making art. Scientists will keep thinking and observing and sharing. Journalists will bear witness.

Keep up the good fight.

February 2017

Dear Mr. President

The idea that President Obama’s policies were bad for jobs is a lie. Robots are bad for jobs. Every time we go through the self-checkout line, computers do the job of a checker. Robots assemble and paint cars. They water plants in greenhouses, check for leaks in pipelines, and diffuse bombs. Those jobs aren’t coming back.

The official (U3) unemployment rate was 7.8% when Obama was sworn into office, on its way up to a high of 9.9%. This was the hand Obama was dealt. Thanks to his policies, the rate was just 4.8% when you took office.

The U6 unemployment rate, which adds in both discouraged workers and workers who choose to work part time, reached a high of 17.1% at the height of the recession, and had dropped to 9.4% at the end of Obama's second term in office.

Whichever set of numbers you use, be consistent.

As for your claim about record crime rates, some actual facts might help.

In 1995, there were 8.2 murders and non-negligent manslaughters per 100,000 people in this country. In 2015, the rate had fallen to 4.9 per 100,000 people.

Now, let's talk about your taxes.

The IRS says that being audited does not prevent you from releasing your taxes. It's clear you just don't want to release them. What are you determined to hide?

And, no, the United States is not a high-tax country. You and GE are proof of that, but here are more numbers.

Measuring taxes as a percentage of GDP, the average rate in developed countries is 34%. We are 32nd out of 35 countries, at 26%. If you want lower taxes, move to Korea, Chile, or Mexico.

Speaking of Mexico...

Considering your history with immigrants, including those who have worked for you, it appears that you're fine with them...if they aren't brown or Muslim.

Immigration over our border with Mexico has been dropping, and is now below net zero. In other words, more people are returning to Mexico than are coming from Mexico. This trend has been going on for some time, perhaps as a result of NAFTA?

If illegal immigrants are taking jobs Americans want, do something about it. 1) Make sure workers, including young men of color, have the education they need to do the jobs that are available. 2) Hold the people who knowingly hire illegal workers responsible.

America has problems. America also has solutions, but isolating ourselves and creating a new class of enemies aren't among them. Neither is whipping up the fury of the less fortunate with lies.

Mr. President, you have a First Amendment right to tell lies.

We, the people, have a duty to call you on them.

February 2017

What Can One Person Do?

At Frank Lucas' recent town hall meeting in Sapulpa, he said, "You come to realize, after you've been through this a while, that folks tend to focus on their day-to-day lives. They come [to town hall meetings] when they're mad or they're scared."

The handful of people who showed up in Sapulpa were mostly concerned about losing their healthcare. I'm thinking a whole lot more of us should be worried enough to show up.

Congressman Markwayne Mullin also held a series of meetings. I guess we can be thankful, in our red state, that Republican legislators aren't afraid to face constituents. However, Mullin made people leave their signs outside the door, and took offense when a woman held up a piece of paper to replace her sign.

In Pryor, a citizen asked him, "What are we going to do to get back to the middle and start taking care of the whole population, not just one side or the other?"

Mullin says, "When constituents act the same way."

Wait! What?

That was the sound of a non-answer, but he was clear in his opinions on the EPA: "I would have never run for office if it wasn't for the fact that my biggest threat to my company was the federal government and the overreach of the EPA."

Dang those clean water requirements!

He wants people to quit demonizing each other, too. He says the American people are tired of it and that's why we have Donald Trump.

"The biggest demonizer of them all!" said someone in the audience, to applause.

Even if I don't agree with much of the platform Mullin and Lucas support, I'm grateful they had the guts to show up. One of our senators doesn't really bother, and the other has replaced town halls with teleconferences. Politicians work for us. Maybe we can remind them if we accept their invitations in numbers and respectfully make our positions known.

We start with common ground. Sure, we all want U.S. corporations to succeed, but our representatives need to know that we want all working people to succeed. Everyone deserves access to healthcare and a living wage.

We believe businesspeople should be heard, but we need to let our representatives know that we want people with no money and no power to be heard, too. That's the promise of this country, and that promise has been broken. It's up to us, the people, one voice, one sign, one town hall meeting at a time. Activism may be all that stands between us and tyranny.

April 2017

Getting Away with Murder

One of my bionic knees doesn't bend as well as the other. I was making progress when insurance coverage for my physical therapy played out. An insurance company employee who didn't know that I'm a miracle walking, a survivor of both polio and osteoarthritis, made the decision based on some corporate chart.

I'm still working on my range of motion at home, but I could have done more with a therapist. I don't want sympathy, I just want you to understand how corporate and political decisions affect the lives of people in Oklahoma.

A lovely lady I know had a stroke. One side is paralyzed, and she can't speak. Of course, she can't work, so we were so happy when her Medicaid came through and she qualified for speech therapy. In a short time, we could see the progress. We could understand more of her words and she was relying less on one-handed signs and left-handed scribbles.

Then the cuts in Medicaid spending started. She lost her therapy. She was resigned. Her friends were angry with the system that lets something like this happen.

Stories like this play out over and over, especially in states that have embraced supply-side economics.

When politicians create policies that make it difficult for constituents to access a good education and affordable healthcare, not only are they chipping away at the economy, they are getting away with murder.

I can't repeat this enough: Trickle down doesn't work. Trickle down isn't fair. Trickle down isn't even remotely Christian.

How many people will die this year because they don't have insurance? How many more will die because we don't have the facilities and the funds to treat mental health issues?

There's a direct correlation between education levels and health. Understanding nutrition, knowing how to read labels, and navigating the healthcare system are all education-related. So, how many lives will be shortened because we shortchange education in favor of corporate donors?

I'm sure there's a mathematician somewhere who has worked out these numbers and charted the cost/earnings ratio. When it comes to the wellbeing of citizens, does it matter?

Robust support systems make people happier and healthier. They help them live longer, more productive lives. We can ignore the science and make laws that benefit a few, lower taxes for oil companies and higher profits for insurance companies. Or we can do the right thing, all of us contributing our fair share, so that all Oklahomans have the chance to live longer, healthier lives.

Doesn't it make sense that we do the right thing?

May 2017

Take the High Road

The man in the White House treats his office as if it were a reality television show. He bars journalists from covering the people's business, trampling on the Bill of Rights as though it were a contract to be negotiated. He incites violence against those with whom he disagrees. Because he doesn't respect the laws of the country, he gives dangerous people permission to disregard both written laws and the laws of humanity.

These are dangerous times, made more dangerous by the lack of civility coming from both sides.

We must respond to attacks on our civil rights, our freedoms, and our safety. But we don't have to resort to name-calling, lying, or deceit. Two wrongs don't make a right. Never has. Never will.

Let's start with language. Does it make us safer to be hateful? Does it accomplish anything to call people names? Okay, a clever tag makes us laugh and relieves tension. But respect must be mutual, and we can't wait for the other side to start.

This administration's malpractice must be making some members of the president's own party sick to their stomachs, but they let it slide because they don't want to lose the votes of their baser base or the blessings of their donors. Letting it slide is evil.

Being respectful doesn't mean we don't stand up and speak up. We can be firm and brave without being disrespectful. And no, Mr. President, respect isn't the same thing as blind loyalty. You don't deserve loyalty when you trample on the rights of the citizens you serve. You don't earn admiration for enriching yourself and your family at the taxpayers' expense.

It is our job, Mr. President, to hold you to the principles embodied in our Constitution. It is the duty of every patriot to point out your misdeeds and the task of journalists to ask hard questions.

You are gifted at stirring the emotional pot. That makes it even more necessary for citizens to educate themselves on the facts and recognize your manipulations.

We will stand up to you. We will defend our country against the likes of you. And we will do so respectfully, not because you have earned it but because it is the right thing to do.

Courtesy and civility will make us stronger as we stand our ground against the tyrants.

June 2017

Pride and Activism

I get it. You believe what you believe and can't understand why I don't believe it, as well. I know, because I can't understand why everyone doesn't agree with my fundamental truths: (1) We are all connected, each part of a greater whole. (2) The creator who created me, created you, too. (3) No single person, book, or religion has a corner on the truth. (4) Diversity makes the system more resilient. (5) Justice for some is not justice at all.

Here's something else I don't understand: two years after the Supreme Court ruled that states could not ban same-sex marriages, two years after friends and family members were able to make their vows legal, why are there people trying to step back progress?

Consider Gertrude Stein and Alice B. Toklas. They met in Paris in 1906. Almost immediately Stein proposed, and Alice accepted. They lived as a committed couple for almost 40 years.

Stein and Toklas collected art, including works by Picasso and Matisse. Stein's will provided for the woman she called her wife. Paintings were to be sold, if necessary, to provide for Toklas' living expenses. Stein's extended family would inherit the remains of the estate on Toklas' death.

That's not what happened. A nephew removed the paintings and placed them in storage. Toklas died twenty years later, penniless, because she didn't have the legal protection of a marriage license.

Imagine being kept from the bedside of a dying partner. Imagine being unable to provide family insurance benefits to the person who shares your life and your home.

We can't go back and set things right, but we must make sure that legal protections stay in place going forward. This requires vigilance.

In 2017, at least eight bills targeting LGBTQ citizens were written by what Freedom Oklahoma Executive Director Troy Stevenson called a "small cabal of bias." Most of the eight bills, written by just three legislators, tried to chip away at marriage equality. All were mean spirited.

As we celebrate the second anniversary of marriage equality, let's commit to activism. Let legislators know that backwards is the wrong direction, because I can assure you that the "cabal of bias" isn't through with its dirty work.

June 2017

Prayer and Charity

Nixon Gage Peters was born with chronic renal failure. At 20 months, he has been approved for a kidney transplant, but the hospital in Oklahoma City won't schedule the surgery until the parents have raised $10,000 for copay and aftercare.

Aftercare is critical. Transplant patients are on a lifetime of anti-rejection medicines. But, with the meds, they have a life—breath, job, family.

Still, it doesn't seem right that a life-saving transplant, as journalist Melanie Payne wrote recently, is being "treated as elective surgery."

Fortunately for little Nixon, his grandmother's work family is trying to raise the money this month. Debbie Pearson has worked at Supplyworks Tulsa for fifteen years. Co-workers have pitched in with a Toro Lawnmower raffle, hotdog stands, street tacos, and change jar contests. They applied for a Homer grant from Supplyworks' parent company, Home Depot, who will match the first 1,667 dollars two for one. They'll still be only halfway there.

Homer grants are funded by and for employees of Home Depot. Workers donate money into the fund, and they apply for funding when there's a need—house fire, accident, kidney transplant.

I am grateful for the good and charitable people in the world, but what a world! What a country that one needs charity to access medical care!

Our needs aren't met until a clerk says they'll be met. As one patient lamented, "My insurance company would rather pay for dialysis three times a week than cover my transplant."

Dialysis is miserable. Treatment for renal failure shouldn't be determined by financial status or an accountant. GoFundMe should be used to send your kid to a tournament or to open a roadside stand, not to access healthcare.

Sadly, GoFundMe for medical treatment has become necessary. Nixon Gage Peters has an account. We raise money online to save lives. Good people contribute. And they form prayer chains. But prayer and charity are not enough!

It's time for good people to rise up and explain to legislators that every life is sacred, even after it's born. Citizens shouldn't have to hold fundraisers for health care. They shouldn't have to beg to save the life of a child. But we do. And we will until our legislators come to their senses.

July 2017

How to Be a Patriot

Drive less and walk more.
No more wars for oil.

Plant a garden.
Teach a child the joy
of dirt.

Adopt a refugee family.
Making friends is cheaper and more reliable
than building walls.

If we are going to build a wall,
let's design it to last
and pay the builders a living wage.
Make sure it can be seen
from outer space.

Include great stone steps
to the top of the wall and down.
Add a Starbucks every quarter mile or so.
Advertise it as a tourist attraction.

Fund science—cures, clean cars, real hover boards.
And space travel.
Someone needs to photograph the wall.

Protect public access
to public lands.

Keep water and air safe
to drink and breathe.

Say no to militants and madmen
who would take for themselves
what belongs to all of us.

Educate everyone.
Feed kids healthy foods.
Pass Medicare for All.

Design libraries to be the most exciting building
in the neighborhood.
Don't leave out poor neighborhoods.

Provide an education
to citizens and guests
in exchange for public service.

Smile at strangers.
Cook meals for the hungry

and the lonely.
Read to a kid.
Coach Little League.
Plant a public orchard.

Stand up for the weak.

Defend the Constitution.

Make music.
Make art.
Make the world a kinder place.

July 2017

This poem appears in *Ain't Gonna Be Treated This Way: Celebrating Woody Guthrie, 2017,* edited by Dorothy Alexander.

It Is Always the Economy

It doesn't matter how clever or even necessary your product is if you don't have the workers who can build it.

You can send your manufacturing to Asia or buy robots. But if American workers are out of a job, who is going to buy your product?

Whether conservatives want to believe it or not, the economy depends on an educated, healthy workforce, not on people just scrambling to get by.

Without workers, no wealth is made. Without consumers, corporations don't prosper. If wages are so low that workers can't afford goods, manufacturers lose. So does the U.S. Treasury.

You can't keep cutting taxes on upper incomes and expect to make up the shortfall with fees on the already cash-strapped middle class. What happens when there is no more middle class?

Comedians and pundits alike made fun of the Democrats' rollout of their new slogan, A Better Deal: Better Jobs, Better Wages, Better Future. Maybe it wasn't catchy, but it captured the spirit of the party.

Democrats know that you can't have social justice without a strong economy.

People are the economy. Democrats need to make this clear. Here are some talking points.

1. Supply-side economics doesn't work. Cutting taxes doesn't generate growth for anyone but the folks at the very top.
2. Unions protect workers. They are the voice of the workers. Robber barons didn't like them. Neither does the GOP.
3. In a capitalistic country, the middle class is the goose. When the goose is dead, there are no more golden eggs.
4. Austerity doesn't make the country great; it makes the citizens desperate.
5. Desperate people are less productive and more dangerous.
6. If the job is necessary to the economy, the wage should be sufficient to feed and house a family.
7. The taxes workers pay should provide for the care and well being of the workers.
8. Building up the military while slashing the domestic budget doesn't make us safer. It just creates conflict on two fronts.
9. A strong military, well funded, is essential, but constant war, cold or otherwise, will bankrupt a country.

The wellbeing of citizens should be the number one issue on any party's agenda. This requires investment. If we can't afford education, health care, national parks, scientific research, and art, we need to raise revenue. In return for the investment, a healthy, educated workforce making decent wages will refill the treasury. This is how you make America great again.

August 2017

Children of the Right Reverend

The wind blowing under the house
lifted the linoleum--
fun house walk in spring,
cold as hell in winter.

Dad's parishioners had no cash for tithes.
We drank raw milk,
made cheese and butter,
canned peaches and green beans,
ate like children of God,

wore handmade clothes
that we hung out on a clothesline.

No Easter dresses,
no prom,
but somehow Mom found money for music,
Dad dug down for books.

Might have qualified for welfare
if we hadn't committed the sin of pride.

Poor, but privileged.
No one ever questioned our promise,
our right to grow up
to be anything.

This poem appeared in *Not a Prodigal*, Poems by Sharon Edge Martin, 2018, and in the *Malpais Review*, Spring, 2016.

Truth, Luck, and Political Correctness

What does politically correct mean, anyway?

I support Black Lives Matter. It has nothing to do with political correctness. My support acknowledges the systemic racism in our country.

Racism isn't dead. Obama isn't responsible for it. And white, straight males have always mattered, especially if they were born lucky, with land, looks, or money.

No one is promoting white guilt, unless, of course, you realize you should feel guilty for marching in, say, a Ku Klux Klan rally or for calling the police because a black delivery person had the nerve to come into your white neighborhood.

Then there's the idea that the far left is as violent as the far right. There is no justification for violence, but are conservatives okay with bullies? How do they feel about folks who don't fight back? Aren't they the ones who passed Stand Your Ground laws and insisted that we all have the right to be armed?

How about the idiotic idea that you can't be both liberal and Christian? Or that one must be a Christian to be a good American?

Public Policy Polling asked Trump supporters, "What religious group do you think faces the most discrimination in America? More than half said Christians, followed by Muslims at 22 percent and Jews at 12 percent. They also believe that whites are the most-discriminated-against racial group.

No political correctness here, just a plate of bull and a side of denial.

Racism exists. We all have biases.

For example, it irritates me when a person answers my, "How are you today?" with, "Blessed." I know it is irrational, but I think, God blessed you, but he sure bailed on that poor dude in the medical helicopter that just flew over.

Luck plays an outsized role in our state of being.
If you are white, the son of a banker and a homemaker, do you have opportunities that the son of a single mother earning minimum wage doesn't?

Do girls have the same opportunities as boys, all else being equal?

What if you're the only child of color in your classroom?

What if your mother speaks Spanish, is in a wheelchair, and is addicted to painkillers?

How do you do homework if your electricity is regularly turned off for nonpayment?

What if you end up in detention at least once or twice a week because you're hungry or can't concentrate in a class of thirty kids?

Our constitution promises justice to people of all faiths, cultures, and skin tones. Speaking out against broken promises isn't left or right. It isn't politically correct. It is just the right thing to do.

August 2017

The New Core

In the last week of my mother's life, Dad was trying to make dinner. As usual, Mom was at his elbow in the kitchen, but my brother knew what to do. He called her into the living room, sat at the piano, and played a song Mom had never heard before. She picked up her guitar and played the song back to him.

My mother was a musician who spent her last sixteen years with dementia. Each little stroke would take more of her memory. At the end, love and music was what she had left. Imagine if she hadn't learned to play and sing.

For this reason and more, music should be part of the core curriculum in every school. There is a body of research that justifies music training; it isn't just personal experience and gut feelings. Music education makes children better thinkers. Musicians recognize patterns; many of them excel in math. And researchers have found that "kids who play an instrument or sing have greater verbal skills."

Brain scans show that musicians have bigger connectors between the two sides of their brains and more gray matter. And if that weren't enough, music can calm or energize. It can affect mood. It can heal.

So can art.

You can't measure creativity with a machine-scored test, but teachers can tell you the value of art in the classroom, from the dirty-hands art of clay and painting to the meditative art of basket weaving. Not only does art teach problem solving, but drawing from life hones observational skills. There's a reason so many scientists are also artists.

If a subject invites a child to see, to listen, or to love to come to school, it belongs in the curriculum.

A whopping majority of Americans, when polled, love the schools their children attend but think schools in general are failing. American schools aren't failing. They reach children of every ability level. They offer services they weren't designed to offer, and they do so with a dedicated and highly educated staff. But years of testing mania and legislative shenanigans have taken a toll.
It's time to get back to what school is about. It's time to pony up the funds, not just for salaries but for programs.

Education should provide students everything they need to choose their futures, as scientists, artists, engineers, construction workers, mechanics, all the jobs that are needed to make civilization work.

School should never be something to dread.

Education isn't just word problems and nonfiction. If it doesn't make students' lives better even into old age, it's time to rethink the core curriculum.

September 2017

Take the Anti-Grover Pledge

If the GOP doesn't pass this tax bill, Vice President Pence said, it will be bad for them in the next election.

If they do pass the GOP tax bill, it will be bad for almost everyone.

Back in Oklahoma, people impacted by our state's tax cuts line up to meet with their lawmakers. The lines stretch out the door and into the street.

When that many people show up to demand action and lawmakers just come up with one more fee, one more tax on the poor and middle class, you have to ask yourself, “Does he (or she) understand what representative means?”

There is a lot of anger seething right now.

Americans have a right to be angry, but for too many citizens, that anger is misplaced. It isn’t immigrants causing the trouble. It isn’t poor people needing help. It isn’t antifa or brown people or uppity woman or those “godless socialists.” It certainly isn’t football players or journalists who ask tough questions.

Corruption is the problem. A regressive tax system…that lets billionaires keep more and gives citizens less…is the problem. Ignoring investments in infrastructure, healthcare, and education in favor of tax breaks is not just dumb, it’s downright unpatriotic.

Ninety percent of us have a right to be angry. Brown people have a right to be angry. Laws target them. Trigger-happy officers shoot first and ask questions later.

Educators have a right to be angry. Schools are overcrowded and understaffed. The curriculum doesn’t serve the students, but it makes a whole lot of money for a couple of testing companies. Even library books are tested.

Middle class families have a right to be angry. Everything has gone up except their income. The safety net has had holes cut in it. Most families require at least two incomes, but the brilliant thinkers in Congress want to take away the Child Care Credit.
The only people getting assistance are corporations and billionaires. Corporations have more rights than we do...and more representation.

In Oklahoma last week, the people who stood in line to see their representatives are our front line. It’s time we stood with them.

It’s also time to join the Anti-Grover Crusade. Let’s take the pledge:

If you cut taxes for the wealthy and services for the poor and middle class, you won’t get our vote.

If you stiff state workers in favor in donors, we will actively campaign against you.

If you cut services for the vulnerable and call it fiscal responsibility, we will call it what it is, hypocrisy.

Taking care of the people's business is patriotic. Hurting citizens in exchange for campaign donations is a form of treason.

October 2017

Where We Are

On the day after Thanksgiving, Americans eat leftovers and buy stuff. It is the leftovers that make the day different from any other, because someone, somewhere, is looking for a way to part you with your money every day of the year.

We worship wealth. Our president has no other qualification for office. Not one. He's mean spirited, and like a lot of manipulators, he's easily manipulated. He is what pure capitalism looks like.

If you don't install brakes on a car, the car will kill you. If we don't install brakes on capitalism, it will kill our country.

We call universal healthcare socialism, and we let people die. They die from lack of preventive care. They die from lack of mental health services. They die because they can't afford to go to the doctor when the sickness is still treatable.

Those who have been conditioned by the word socialism keep on voting for the most expensive, most rationed healthcare in the industrialized world.

We call public education a liberal plot. When only rich people's kids are educated, we will have a third world country, the dark ages, nobles and serfs.

When only those who can afford their own lawyers have access to justice, there is no justice. Repeat after me: Justice for some is not justice at all.

Only those who already believe this are still reading. Too many have bought into the lies that allow plutocrats to squeeze out every last dime from the citizens and destroy the dream that the founders had for this country.

Dishonest politicians parrot what people want to hear and they believe them, regardless of how the politicians act. How many sociopaths get votes from the people they hurt just by calling themselves Christians?

"We will know they are Christians by their love," the song goes.
I'm hearing the words, but I'm not seeing the love.

When people lose what they have left, who will they blame? I'm betting they won't blame themselves for not listening to actual journalists, economists, or reason.

November 2017

The Family Values Party

In the richest country in the world, a family should have a roof over its head, food on the table, and access to education and healthcare. Safety, justice, and sound economic policies are family values, not those button-pushing issues with which politicians distract voters as they line their own pockets.

Take the matter of Planned Parenthood.

Planned Parenthood clinics offer essential services, especially to people without access to preventive care. The clinics offer education and contraception, the two main drivers in reducing both unwanted pregnancies and abortions.

In red states, GOP majorities have been shutting down Planned Parenthood clinics, making it more difficult for low-income women to get IUDs and contraceptive implants. Meanwhile, in blue New Jersey, the number of clinics has risen and the number of women getting abortions has fallen.

So, if not to reduce abortions, what's the real reason Republicans want to shut down Planned Parenthood?

For what purpose do they erase the gains made by the Affordable Care Act? Who benefits if a state doesn't expand Medicaid? It certainly isn't the poor and uninsured. Who gains if the Children's Healthcare Insurance Program isn't funded? It isn't low-income families.

Universal healthcare is a family value.

Education is a family value.

More than half the marriages among those without a high school diploma end in divorce. The divorce rate drops to about 30 percent if couples have college degrees.

Educated people are more likely to raise children in two-parent households.

Educated people live longer, healthier lives.

The GOP tax scam that taxes tuition wavers as income will close doors on education to all but the wealthy. Expanding education opportunities, whether it is graduate school or trade school, is a family values issue.

Since *Roe v. Wade*, the percentage of white, middle class women seeking abortions has dropped. But with stagnate wages and a shrinking middle class, abortions have risen among the poor, including poor people of color.

Raising wages so families can afford to raise children is a family value.

One of the biggest cons that Republicans have pulled on voters is that you can't be a Christian and vote Democrat.

If your legislator claims to be a Christian, tell them you want actions and not just words. "By their deeds you shall know them." If he or she votes against programs that support families, let them know they won't get your vote.

Democrats are the real party of family values. It's time they hone their message and make this clear.

December 2017

How Democracy Fails

Mitch McConnell and Paul Ryan take from the poor and give to the rich without flinching. It's not that they don't like little people; we just don't matter.

Republicans know they have the power, and they plan to do everything they can while they can to cement it for the next generation. Only one party matters, and we can't just blame Putin.

Did Russia interfere with the election? U.S. intelligence agencies say so, but this coup didn't happen in just one election cycle.

On December 9, 2000, the Supreme Court halted the recount in Florida and on December 12 declared George W. Bush winner of the election. The real prize was redistricting. The GOP redrew voting districts and gave election security to party members all the way down into state and local jurisdictions.

Two war fronts when one might have been winnable, tax cuts in wartime, banks too big to fail, and home loans for which lenders had no responsibility crashed the economy in 2008. Young people voted for hope, but the party that lost declared they weren't going to have it.

In 2010, the Supreme Court called money free speech. Now elections were easier to buy. And in 2013, SCOTUS undid a key section of the Voting Rights Act. Now states were free to demand special IDs, shorten voting hours, and otherwise keep undesirables from the polls.

For eight years, there was constant effort to undermine President Obama. Why? His policies brought us out of the worst recession since the Great Depression. We weren't afraid of nuclear annihilation, either.

Sore losers refused to vote on judges nominated to fill vacant seats. Legislators demanded concessions then refused to vote for the Affordable Care Act. They cared more for their donors--insurance companies, banks, and billionaires—than they did for the health and wellbeing of the people they swore to serve.

They undermined the president with lies and innuendos despite the esteem in which he was held by the rest of the world. And in 2016, even when McConnell and others knew of Russian interference and hacking, they stood in the way of letting the American people know.

This is treason in my book. And the resulting damage will likely be catastrophic.

Remember the Dow losing over half its value? This hit retirees especially hard. Pre-existing conditions made you uninsurable. Now, even children are in danger of losing coverage that once had bipartisan support.

Dreamers are looking over their shoulders while Vice President Pence has his own dreams of a nation as cleansed of non-Christians as Myanmar is of Rohingya Muslims.

With the constant attack on the press, intelligence agencies, and truth, we can become just another dictatorship by committee. Or party.

This isn't patriotism; it's a coup. The framers of our Constitution must be spinning in their graves.

January 2018

Not Quite Armageddon

A tax bill should be about improving the economy of the country and the well being of the citizens. Instead, the GOP has made it about greed and retaliation.

1. The bill was created behind closed doors with no conversation at all with the Democrats.
2. While Democrats were not allowed to contribute to the bill, you can bet your bottom that they will be blamed for not voting for it.
3. Provisions that hurt high-tax states, states which use those taxes to educate and care for their citizens, were put into the bill expressly to hurt the Democratic legislators in those states.
4. While the bill may hurt those legislators, the provisions actually hurt the citizens in those states. They pay taxes that they cannot write off. This was done on purpose…for political purpose.

5. If GOP legislators hurt the citizens to score a point, if they hurt citizens to reward their wealthy donors, if they hurt citizens for their own gains, why would you vote for them ever again?
6. This single example of political retaliation only scratches the surface of the damage this tax bill will do.
7. And yet, despite the lies and the damage, the GOP base still supports its legislators.
8. Yep, we are all up the creek. You know which creek.

January 2018

Sick and Tired

I'm tired of mean, self-serving politicians,
of talking points and propaganda.
of pols and pundits manipulating citizens
with words, half lies, and outright fabrications.

The people in Puerto Rico are tired. Even if someone has explained to the president that Puerto Ricans are citizens, it doesn't seem to have done any good.

Dreamers are tired. They are tired of having their dreams dashed, of looking over the shoulders, of leaving behind their families.

Journalists are tired. The would-be despot understands quite well that this institution stands between despots and free people. Their jobs have gotten so much harder and more dangerous in the past year.

Parents are tired. Working parents who live close to the bone are worried that their children won't have access to healthcare. Why was funding for the Children's Health Insurance Program allowed to lapse? Does it have anything to do with its champion?

Who thought that Children's Health Insurance was a suitable bargaining chip anyway? Whoever made that decision, shame on you!

We are all tired of arguing with people who have made up their minds that only one side is right. Compromise and center are not dirty words.

As our country descends into chaos, some of us are more than just tired. We're frightened. We're concerned not only for ourselves but for friends and relatives who think everything is okay so long as their side is winning.

No one is winning, especially when one party has all the power. We are not okay.

Is this even a democratic republic anymore?

January 2018

Closing Our Doors

This administration does not want your tired or your hungry. The president could care less that you are fleeing from persecution. If you're brown, willing to work, and are paying taxes on your income, that doesn't hold the door open for you.

In the State of the Union message, the president commended those Americans who, building lives "between the ocean and the wilderness," fought for freedom. He didn't say that those brave folk were immigrants, many of them fleeing persecution. There was no mention of the people who were already here when they arrived.

While the door is being slammed shut, the president and his advisors stoke your fears. Refugees are their favorite targets.

If your government were killing its own citizens, wouldn't you try to get your family out of harm's way? Wouldn't you try to find a safe place to go?

Young men cross borders, live in horrid conditions, suffer beatings and jail, but they don't give up. Families struggle to save their young children. Children of immigrants who make it to safety learn new languages and adapt despite the trauma of their young lives.

Aren't these the very humans the human race needs? Evolution favors adaptors, problem solvers, the brave, the thinkers and doers. These are our ancestors, those who came across the Bering land bridge and those who sailed across the ocean. These are the people our president and too many conservative leaders fear. They don't want thinkers and doers; they want unquestioning followers.

There is also unabashed racism in their platform. The "shithole countries" comment that made its way to the public was a rare moment of truth for this president.

Already, babies of color outnumber white babies in the U.S. By 2020, children of color will outnumber white children in elementary schools. It appears that this scares the GOP.

Not all conservatives are racists, but the racist right fought President Obama on issues that they would have supported if he'd just been a white man. They want you to be afraid of children fleeing violence in Central America. They want you to believe that Green Cards are handed out without oversight and that allowing a family to bring their elderly parents to this country is a danger.

They want you to be afraid because they are afraid. They aren't afraid of terrorism nearly as much as they are afraid of losing their entitlement.

Perhaps the scariest moment in the president's speech came when he suggested that a "major event" was the only way to bring America together. It was almost palpable, that feeling of needing an attack to cement his power.

Not only could he unite the country in common horror, he'd have the very excuse he needs to lock the doors. Let's pray he doesn't start a war to get what he wants.

February 2018

The Need for Critical Thinkers

For the same reason that some legislators refuse to do what is necessary to adequately fund public education, it was once illegal to teach a slave to read.

Those who seek power and their own interests fear educated citizens. They want pawns, not critical thinkers. Critical literacy is necessary for a free society.

Without an education system that includes everyone, justice is impossible.

Justice for some is not justice.

Economic security for some is not economic security.

A healthcare system that leaves people out is neither just nor economically viable.

Incarceration as a means to shape society is a travesty. So are for-profit prisons.

Critical thinkers understand these things. They question legislators and administrations that seek to curtail our right to question them. They demand the right to speak out against corruption. They insist on every citizen's right to vote.

Facts are essential. Finding the facts requires good research skills and the ability to tell truths from lies.

Here's a fact: the push to arm teachers is troubling.

Parents with critical thinking skills don't want weapons in the classroom. If teachers are armed, thinking parents who can afford to do so will take their kids out of public schools. Those who aren't homeschooled will be enrolled in private schools where weapons are not allowed. This will be another blow to public education funding.

It's time to think, folks. Don't let gun manufacturers think for you. A good shotgun will keep the varmints away. A hunting rifle, most as lethal as any military weapon, will keep your family fed.
A pistol by your bedside may or may not keep your family safe. Here's another fact: more gun deaths occur in homes that have guns.

Let's change laws to protect people from shoot-first law enforcement. Let's stop manufacturers from selling military weapons to the general public.

Arming teachers is not the solution. Militarizing the police force is not the solution.

Arming students with critical thinking skills is.

We must make sure public schools stay open, and we must improve access to mental health treatment. Tell your legislators to pass sensible regulations.

Your Second Amendment rights are safe. Let's make sure the rest of our Constitution and our children are, too.

February 2018

High Cost of Being Mean

Our president has a history of reneging on contracts. Cheating contractors isn't the act of a kind person. Neither is cheating on wives and girlfriends.

He lies so often that major newspapers in the country track and archive his lies. One fact checker says 70 percent of the president's statements are false.

It's safe to say, he's a cheat and a liar.

He's also thin-skinned and vengeful, willing to destroy others to save himself. So, we should not be surprised that he fired Andrew McCabe two days before McCabe was set to retire.

The president ended the DACA program and expects us to think it is someone else's fault. The way he has treated Dreamers and long-time residents ranks at the top of the meanness scale. He tears families apart, and he breaks down the morale of the whole country.
He's mean. It's ridiculous that party members still support him. If you're still a fan of the president you are okay with his meanness, but you can't call yourself a fiscal conservative.

States that invest more in education have a higher per capita income. Not only is equality in education kind, it's a good investment. Privatizing education will not save money and it will not give superior results.

Universal healthcare is kind and financially sound. Herd immunity makes the whole herd stronger. Universal healthcare is cheaper. And it delivers superior results.

Out of ten industrialized countries, the U.S. comes in last on health results and first in amount of money spent. That's neither fiscally conservative nor kind.

Perhaps the cruelest thing our lawmakers have done is privatize prisons.

Even before we started guaranteeing private prisons a certain occupancy rate, lawmakers engineered laws to control minority populations. There is a reason so many black males end up behind bars.

Guaranteeing an occupancy rate also guarantees that those who rely on the support of prison corporations for campaign donations will be "tough on crime."

Incarceration instead of education, treatment, and rehabilitation is not only more costly to the taxpayer, but it costs families.

Breadwinners behind bars can't earn a living. Children of the incarcerated suffer most and are more likely to end up in prison themselves. This, from the party of family values!

Our refusal to give safe harbor to refugees is unkind. And senseless. Immigrants, both the highly educated and those just looking for a chance to support their families, have contributed to the prosperity and wellbeing of the country. Fear and hate have failed.

Let's give humane policies a chance.

March 2018

Corruption Is the Problem

The voices of the people can't be heard over the thunderclaps of corruption and propaganda.

When money buys legislation, that's corruption.

When money buys the message and the messenger, that's propaganda.

If you want to make an ultra-conservative really mad, just tell her that George Soros is behind a piece of legislation. This week, Soros was accused of paying millions of marchers.

If you have a problem with Soros but are fine with the Koch brothers and Harold Hamm writing legislation for Oklahoma, you have succumbed to propaganda poisoning.

Propaganda is a potent tool in a corrupt state. It allows corrupt politicians to pass corrupt laws without losing their voting base. Misinformed voters allow corporations and billionaires to avoid paying their fair share of the taxes that provide services for everyone.

The Founding Fathers weren't saints, and they weren't always right on the issues, including slavery, but they created a Constitution that has lasted and evolved for more than 200 years. Thanks to a handful of Supreme Court Justices, corruption, and propaganda, the Constitution is in jeopardy.

Citizens United, which allows corporations and certain other entities to spend unlimited amounts of money to sway elections, legalized corruption. What's more, too much of what is spent is dark money. We don't even know where it's coming from.

When a handful of media outlets control the message, the formula is complete. Fool the voters. They don't notice that their own legislators have been bought so long as they are afraid that your legislators have been.

While students are marching and you are fretting over the latest conspiracy theory, the legislature is free to pass laws in the dead of night that bear no resemblance to what you were promised or what voters need.

Lobbyists, like voters, should have the right to speak. What they don't deserve is the right to control the conversation. They don't have the right to buy legislators. Neither do billionaires and corporations.

There are plenty of things that need to be fixed in this country, but until we tackle the problem of corruption, nothing will be fixed but elections.

Let's rally for an overturn of *Citizens United.* Let's fight for free and fair elections. Let's stand for the right of every single eligible voter to vote. Then we can actually tackle things that matter—justice, infrastructure, education, access to healthcare, gun violence, and living wages.

April 2018

Dear Governor

We understand that you don't have much respect for teachers. If you did, there would be no need for teachers to march. You don't seem to understand why education is so important, either, judging from your recent remarks. Seriously, testing time is no more important than any other time of the year unless you have bought into the corporate lies about million-dollar testing programs.

Testing can tell you about a district's socioeconomic status. Test scores can tell you if a student is good at taking tests. Tests measure confidence, decoding skills, and vocabulary. Alas, they don't really measure math skills. A math whiz with dyslexia is just out of luck. I know, because I've given tests every year of my teaching life.

Tests do not measure creativity. They don't measure tenacity. They don't say one thing about what a child has gone through to get where he or she is. They might measure growth, but if it starts from nothing and gets to somewhere less than superior, it doesn't seem to count. Testing money would be so much better spent on libraries and librarians, math labs, and field trips.

Governor, you can't cut taxes and starve services and expect golden results. We need for you and your party to take responsibility and find solutions to the mess you've created.

April 2018

Deadly Ideology

Extreme divides are deadly. More than six hundred thousand American soldiers died in the fight over slavery and states' rights. Even after Robert E. Lee gave up his sword at Appomattox, the South continued its ideological fight. Forty acres, a mule, and commitment to human rights would have solved a host of problems, but the South and the supremacists dug in their heels. They are still digging. And they're not just in the South anymore.

They do this under the banner of conservatism.

What are they trying to conserve? The racial divide? Second-class citizenship? A ruling class? The power of rich white males?

Money?

Today's self-described fiscal conservatives aren't. They give away huge sums to corporations and the wealthy while complaining about investments in health and education that actually return money to the treasury. No matter how many times a recession follows a big tax cut, they just have to try it one more time.

Investment is fiscally conservative. Giveaways to cronies and pet causes are not.

Are they trying to conserve a power structure of some sort? Of course. No one gives up advantage easily.

In their struggle to maintain the flawed status quo, people on both sides of the aisle are dying. They're dying of addictions that aren't treated. They're dying of preventable diseases.

Immigrants are sent back into war zones.

Human rights are violated. What are the long-term consequences of snatching children from their parents? What kind of world are we shaping with this hideous turn?

Families here at home are broken apart because of a sexist, racist, classist, underfunded corrections system. What are the long-term effects of incarcerating mothers and fathers instead of treating addictions and addressing the root causes of poverty?

America has never been a perfect union, but we can sure do a lot better than we have been doing lately. Let's reclaim real conservatism and conserve the living, breathing document that is our Constitution. Let's conserve the spirit of independence. Let's refuse to bow to a king or to a ruling ideology.

It is time to get off the ideological bandwagon and come together to find solutions. I pray it isn't too late.

June 2018

Real Patriots

We are a country of laws. The past few weeks, friends and relatives have been telling me this when I point out that separating children from their parents is a human rights violation. I can only assume that at least some of these law-abiding citizens are pot smokers or speedy drivers, but we're not talking irony here. We're talking justice.

Laws are made to serve the people, not people to serve the laws. What good is law and order if the laws are unjust?

Your friends spouting conservative talking points about law and order are the same ones who claim kinship with the patriots in fake Indian costumes who tossed tea into Boston Harbor. They forget that the original patriots were rebels, protesting injustice.

I'm not sure I would have thrown tea into the harbor. Seems a boycott would have worked. Besides, I have a natural aversion to waste and to white people deflecting blame onto brown people.

I also have an aversion to unjust laws.

If my child had seizures that could be stopped with illegal THC, you can bet your buttons that I'd ignore an illogical drug law and treat my child. A child's life should trump the law.

Laws can be manipulated to make a point.

By choosing to charge parents who cross the border illegally, the president's henchmen set up a situation that allowed them to separate children from their parents. They could just as easily make it simple for families to ask for asylum.

Law and order people seem to have no problem ignoring laws they don't like.

Remember when Mary Fallin refused to accept the law that expanded Medicaid in this state? How many people are still dying too soon because they don't have health insurance?

Remember when we, the people of Oklahoma, overwhelmingly passed a state question that would restructure sentencing in Oklahoma? The law and order folk got busy on legislation to subvert the will of the people. How many citizens are still in prison on nonviolent offenses when they, their families, and the state would be better served by commonsense reforms?

Hitler and his party were able to commit atrocities because the people accepted unjust laws. Bless the folk who broke the law and hid or helped to escape those deemed undesirable by the Nazis.

America is a country of laws. We are also a country of citizens who like to call themselves patriots. Real patriots take to the streets and the harbors. Real patriots understand sanctuary and stand up to a nationalist administration. Real patriots refuse to follow unjust laws.

July 2018

Lines for My Friend, Sandy, Who Wanted a Lighthearted Poem

It's hard to be lighthearted
when your president's a liar,
when the whole dang world is threatened
by his pants that are afire.

He shreds the Constitution
and feeds it to the rats,
rules by whim and fiat

and blames the Democrats.

To think, he used to be one!
But then the party turned.
No longer segregationist!
The Jim Crow laws all burned,

at least in legal rule books.
We know Jim Crow's still here,
and the liar's words and actions
stir up the racists' fears.

Adored by evangelicals.
I can't imagine why.
This preacher's kid knows Christians,
and this hater comes up shy.

He's stacking courts with corporatists
undoing revolution.
We shed the aristocracy once.
This backward evolution

should not sit well with patriots,
and that's us, do you hear,
the workers and the poets,
the brown folk and the queer,

moms and dads, day laborers,
all those who earn a wage,
who vote and pay their taxes,
the ignorant and the sage.

We're all in this together
We all must march and shout
and call and vote and rally.
We can't sit this one out.

Here's hoping there is justice
and it lands his butt in jail.
Do you believe in karma?
Will Putin go his bail?

July 2018

Can We, Please, Make America Great Again?

The Greek statesman, Pericles, had a word for people who don't educate themselves politically or make an effort to vote: useless. Citizens, he said, were "fair judges of public matters" and bring "daring and deliberation" to politics. He saw an Athenian "who takes no part in these duties not as unambitious but as useless."

Non-voters are not just useless, they're dangerous.

Secretary Clinton won the popular vote, but in those swing states, what if everyone had voted? If a candidate's approval rating is in the 30s and 40s and everyone votes, is there a way he or she can win?

It's also important that every vote be counted!

In the past few months we've seen just how quickly the democratic order can collapse. When the president and his henchmen commit to a full-out war on truth, equality, and human rights, and when the checks and balances that have worked for more than 200 years are undermined or ignored, it is a short, steep slope to dictatorship.

Where are Congress and the Senate in all this? Is the GOP really ready to give away our democracy just for the right to confirm one more corporatist Supreme Court Justice? It would seem so.

Mitch McConnell has already shown his colors by refusing to allow a vote on Merrick Garland, a well-regarded centrist. It's activist judges or nothing, if I may quote the far right.

Before it is too late, we must vow that we won't be useless. Encourage friends and neighbors to vote. But, first, do no harm!

Educate yourself on the candidates and the issues. Candidates come with a history. Know that history before you vote.

I can't believe half of U.S. voters are willing to sit this next election out, allow one party to transfer the wealth and the power of this country to a handful of citizens, and let a dictator wannabe destroy the progress of 200-plus years.

America has never been perfect. We don't have to forgive the religious intolerance, the sexism, and the racism. Instead, we look to the sound principles created for rich, white men that are gradually, usually after a hard fight, being offered to the rest of us.

Forget originalism. When the Constitution was written, women and Africans were property. Instead, we must protect what the Constitution has become and is becoming before we lose everything to hatred, greed, and the psychopath in the White House.

Elections have consequences. Vote, dammit!

And know for what and for whom you're voting!

July 2018

Who Is the Real Conservative?

You don't give tax breaks to the people who already have all the money.

You don't collect money from the citizens and give it to corporations.

If you think these are good ideas, you cannot call yourself a conservative. There's nothing conservative about blowing money up the chute from the working poor to corporations and billionaires.

If you work for wages and you vote for candidates who promise to cut taxes, you've been conned into making the rich richer at your expense.

If you buy into the idea that estates worth more than five million dollars should be exempt from paying an estate tax, you've been conned into creating, over generations, a moneyed aristocracy.

Like all good cons, you won't realize you've been swindled at first. Take the massive tax cut passed by the GOP and signed by President Trump. They doubled the standard deduction. A lot of us will benefit from that.

But here's a short list of what we have already lost or are likely to lose when you cut taxes on top earners:

services for veterans
classrooms with a teachable number of students
libraries and librarians in every school
drinkable water from the tap
safe roads and bridges
access to health care
access to mental health care
rural hospitals
nursing homes and elder care
accessible post office hours
real people on the phone when you need to call the IRS

Conservatives invest money. True conservative politicians invest money in the people they serve. They give a hand up to the poor—education and training, health and wellbeing—so they, too, can become contributors. They don't give it to folks who buy yachts then register them in the Cayman Islands so they don't have to pay property tax on them.

If you don't get this, there's a good chance you've been swindled by politicians who only claim to be conservatives. So, save the extra in your paycheck from that doubled standard deduction. You'll need it when your pre-existing condition is no longer covered.

It will be too late when Medicare and Social Security have been privatized.

August 2018

How Did We Get Here?

There are a lot of things I don't understand. I don't get how sound waves are captured and transmitted. I'm baffled by batteries. But what astounds me most is how people make decisions about which politicians to trust.

Here's what I know is coming every time I bring up the number of lies told by the president:

(1) all politicians lie, or
(2) remember when Bill Clinton said "it depends on what the definition of *is* is" or
(3) remember when Barack Obama said, "If you like your policy you can keep your policy."

It's telling that the examples used are always the same ones. I mean, how could you choose which of President Trump's lies to use as an example when they now number in the thousands.

Why do people stand by him, a proven liar? Is it possible that nationalism is at the heart of all this? Are people so afraid that white, male Christians are no longer going to be in command of every institution that they must lie to themselves?

It's possible. This state still hasn't signed the Equal Rights Amendment.

I keep hoping that common sense and goodness prevail, that my friends and neighbors come to believe that the world is big enough for everyone in it. If we share.

Yes, we're overpopulated. Humans multiply, but war and closed doors won't fix the problem. In fact, they make most of them. What are the answers?

Education and access to healthcare are essential. Educated women have fewer children. Access to healthcare insures that the children who are born are more likely to survive.

Humanitarian aid makes us strong. Diplomacy is more effective than war. Kindness is strength. Community and justice aren't dirty words.

We are all one human race, and every creature on this planet has a place. The bottom of the food chain is just as important as the top. Kill the plankton and you kill the whale.

It's time to come to the center, time to find workable solutions that don't just benefit the right or the left, the rich or the poor, the native or the immigrant. And it's time to call out evil wherever we find it.

Corruption and evil are corrupt and evil, even if you voted for it.

September 2018

Who Gives Them the Right?

Making abortion illegal doesn't make abortion go away, it just makes it dangerous. If we strip women of their right to choose, and if we close safe abortion clinics, we return to the bad old days of back alleys and coat hangers.

If you aren't pro-choice, please don't call yourself pro-life.

Now, let's get into solutions. How do we make abortions as rare as they should be?

First, education. Public schools and quality sex education programs are the first line of defense against unwanted pregnancies and spreadable diseases.

If you want your children and their children to have the best possible chance in life, make sure they get an education before they have to make tough choices about dropping out of school or giving up a baby for adoption.

Second, we can reduce unwanted pregnancies among all populations by making condoms and other contraceptives both available and affordable.

Third, let's make sure there are resources to protect young people in dangerous situations. Legislators, fund schools well enough that school counselors and nurses are available for every child and not just those in high-rent districts.

Fourth, healthcare for everyone! Universal healthcare should include discussions with medical personnel about sex if that is more comfortable for you and your child. And it should absolutely include contraceptives.

Fifth, let's pay workers a living wage. The ability to feed and educate a child and to pay for childcare figures in childbirth decisions.

The rights of women to choose when and if they become mothers will be just another good-old-days story if Vice President Pence, Judge Kavanaugh and all those who beat the pro-life drums get their way. If they were really pro-life, that is, pro every single life, this discussion wouldn't be necessary. But they aren't and it is.

Let's take this discussion to the streets.

September 2018

Yes, Mr. President, We're Devastated

A handful of powerful men think women are the problem. How dare any female dredge up old misdeeds, including attempted rape, to ruin a powerful man?

The President of the United States says he doesn't believe there are women devastated by the confirmation of Brett Kavanaugh to the Supreme Court.

Trust us, Mr. President. We're devastated. And why shouldn't we be!

According to RAINN (Rape, Abuse, & Incest National Network), of 1000 rapes, only 310 are reported. Of those 310 reports, 57 result in arrests and six rapists are incarcerated. Yes, six prison sentences out of 1000 rapes!

Why don't more rape victims report? There are more reasons for not reporting than there are prison sentences per 1000 abusers, including fear, no expectation of justice, vilification of victims, and a patriarchy afraid of losing power.

If you were young and you were told it was all your fault, what would you do?

What if your rapist threatened to kill you if you talked?

Maybe your abuser is someone you've been taught to trust. Who would believe you?

If the President of the United States, in front of television cameras and a crowd, makes fun of someone who tells her story, would that make you feel safe enough to speak?

If he orders a sham investigation into the accused, who is later sworn in as a Justice of the Supreme Court, would you be willing to put yourself at risk to speak up?

Maybe silence is the goal.

We must not be silenced.

Yes, one is innocent until proven guilty. But victims who speak up must be taken seriously until they are proven to be lying. That requires real investigations.

It takes courage to speak. Until women who speak get the respect they deserve, it requires the courage of all of us to stand with them, to demand investigations, to demand that rape kits be tested, to demand justice.

Many voices and many activists have more power than a few old men who care more for their own power than they do for the people they serve.

October 2018

What Do We Do Now?

My cousin thinks climate change is "bogus theology made up by liberals." When I disputed his claim that there were "just as many examples on the other side as on the warming side," he called my response "an example of liberal disenfranchisement."

Disenfranchisement? Merriam-Webster defines it as "the state of being deprived of a right or privilege, especially the right to vote."

Our vote is our voice. Is this what he meant?

No. He finally came to the real reason he doesn't believe in global warming: "I don't believe there is anything short of all out nuclear war that man can do to upset the system God put in place."

How do we counter someone's theology? Why would God not want us to control carbon emissions?

Science is neither liberal nor conservative. It isn't anti-religion. If someone is trying to make you think it is, be wary of motives.

That's not saying that there isn't shoddy science. A huckster can do a lot of damage before he's found out. The doctor who claimed there was a link between vaccines and autism is a case in point. Although he lost his license to practice medicine, there are still children who get preventable diseases as a direct result of his unsubstantiated claims.

Good science doesn't rely on anecdotes. It's reproducible, and it welcomes the effort, but know who funds the research and who stands to gain or lose based on the results.

An important, and frightening, report about climate change was released this month. The strongest hurricane to ever hit the panhandle of Florida added its two cents to the report. Despite the scientists and the storms, our president says he doesn't believe in global warming or in scientists who all have a political agenda.

Can 97 percent of the world's climate scientists be wrong? I suppose it is possible. There was a time when most doctors and barbers relied on leeches to treat patients. But global water and air temp measurements are fact. So are rising oceans. So are lost beaches and islands. Catastrophic weather events are more frequent and more catastrophic.

So what are we going to do, despite the president's policies, despite his deep-pocketed backers? We're going to work together, speak up together, and educate ourselves about the issues. We will vote in every election while we still can. And we must change our own habits, which may be the hardest thing of all.

October 2018

Hope and Change, 2018

I'm white,
healthy,
comfortable
with my middle-class trappings,
but today your despair is my despair,

Child taken at the border,
orphaned by deportation.

Refugees
from violence and hunger,
willing to chance
a thousand-mile journey, starting
with nothing.

My friend's transgender son,
a veteran
the president wants to erase.

Black folk
and poor folk
who can't vote
because it's not in some rich, white dude's
best interest.

A country ruled
by a minority
who will do whatever it takes,
including cheat,
to keep power,
and I'm all out of hope.

Selfish of me,
because my feelings
can't compare
with your despair,
and shouldn't.

Hopelessness can fix nothing,
but our votes can.

The Deadliest Sin

It's a common joke in our house when something doesn't get done: "The owner of this establishment is not responsible."

The more I see of my fellow humans (and of myself) the more I realize that humans are pretty irresponsible creatures. The term "humanity" doesn't always have positive connotations. And America hasn't built a shining city on the hill.

We have contributed to the starvation (a gruesome death) of 85,000 children under the age of five in Yemen. The money earned by our war machine is more important than these children's lives, so how can we be surprised that the president is unmoved by the premeditated murder of one journalist.

As horrific as all this is, the administration's willingness to undo any steps toward slowing climate change will contribute to ever greater horror in the next hundred years.

It is impossible for anyone in the state of Florida to believe that climate change isn't happening, yet here is a man at Mar a Lago who claims that climate change is uncertain. Whether he truly believes this or is just using the uncertainty as a political tool is the only thing uncertain. That so many people in this country do not believe climate change is settled science is testament to the power of mass brainwashing.

Greed and lust for power are the force behind this mass public relations campaign. In fact, oil company scientists were among the first to understand the effects on the climate of burning fossil fuels. And they were the first to adopt a policy of misinformation.

The same policy was adopted in the 2000 presidential campaign. A memo written by a Bush advisor, Frank Lutz, said, "Voters believe that there is no consensus about global warming within the scientific community. Should the public come to believe that the scientific issues are settled, their views about global warming will change accordingly. Therefore, you need to continue to make the lack of scientific certainty a primary issue in the debate."

To this day, Al Gore is an object of derision in Oklahoma for speaking the truth.
Greed wins, and it is a loss for all of humanity, both the good and the bad of it. Because of war and climate change the number of refugees will only grow. How we treat this planet, how we treat the truth, and how we treat those who must leave their homes depends on what kind of people we are. And it is up to each of us to do what's right, because in Oklahoma and the U.S., our leaders are not responsible.

November 2018

Scrabbling for Hope

This administration isn't as bad as I thought it would be; it's much worse. A Soviet-style dictator and an autocratic crown prince direct the president, whether by flattery or by what they hold over him. Putin applauds as we pull out of Syria. Mohammed bin Salman gets away with murder.

A troll farm spreads chaos, and the president tries to stop the investigation into Russian interference because it casts a shadow on his "big win," an electoral college win orchestrated by big data and internet trolls and abetted by gerrymandering and curtailed voting rights.

On the news recently, a mouth for the administration explained why they were rolling back civil rights protections for students of color who are much more likely than other students to be suspended or sent to detention.

"These people," she said, "come to school with issues."

I don't suppose it occurred to her that addressing the issues of poverty and second-rate education might be more just, never mind more economically sound.

She also cited school safety as the main reason for the suspension numbers.

So, we have to kick brown kids out of school to keep young, white males from shooting up the place?

More than civil rights are being rolled back.

The nationalist in the White House can't let stand any progress made by the black statesman that preceded him, even if it destroys the country. Even if it destroys the planet. Even if it pushes Iran closer to nuclear weapons. Even if it dashes all hope for a two-state solution in what was once Palestine. Even if children are orphaned by our immigration policies. Or tear gassed. Even if it destroys NATO and the European Union that stymie Putin's ambitious plans to remake the Soviet Union.

Where's the hope in all this? We, the people, are the hope.

We took back the House in November, but that isn't enough. We have to keep standing up to the bully standing behind the biggest bully pulpit of them all. We have to protect the weak, protest the shredding of our Constitution, and keep on keeping on.

The only antidote to this toxic administration is our action. The wannabe dictator and his handlers won't win because we won't let them.

Here's wishing all of us hope and strength for the fight in the coming year.

December 2018

Reality TV President

In case you haven't figured it out, our president doesn't give a fig about the people he swore to serve. He detests anyone who speaks out against him. He uses the people who voted for him, who attend his rallies, who still defend his ill-begotten policies.

If you're a member of his base, you must know he used you in the midterms to defeat members of his own party who opposed him. He's using you now to make himself feel better about what he's doing to the country, what he's doing to the world. He's not making anyone's life better. We're not safer. We're not more prosperous. And things are going to get much worse if he's allowed to continue his rampage.

Let's start with the border wall lie. He knew that Mexico wouldn't pay for it. He didn't think the lie mattered, because he didn't think he'd be president. With his creepy debates and the international attention a run for the presidency gave him, he was looking for another television series. Well, he got one.

If you're still unsure of this, think about the baseless fear he stirred up about refugees, about his total lack of compassion. People don't take a thousand mile journey by foot through a desert unless they're all out of other options.

Think about National Guard soldiers who missed Thanksgiving and Christmas with their families so they could string concertina wire along the southern border. Think about Customs and Border Patrol agents who are working without pay because the president goes back on his promises.

There was a deal. The president changed his mind. A year or so ago, he had the five billion for a border wall in exchange for legislation to protect the Dreamers. He changed his mind.

He doesn't care about the Dreamers, one way or another. Dreamers are just a negotiating tool.

He doesn't care if you have access to healthcare.

He doesn't care (and he doesn't know) what the Constitution says.

He doesn't care if his policies deprive farmers of their livelihood.

He doesn't care if the stock market tanks. When that happens, billionaires can pick up bargains. Retirees who are living off their 401ks can go to hell.

So here's the deal: Democrats in the House should offer the president five billion dollars to hire more border patrol agents and train them, to hire enough immigration judges to clear the backlog of asylum seekers, and to put high tech surveillance equipment in remote places.

The money must be used to make us safer, not to make a statement. And if walls are needed at high-volume areas, then, let's build those walls. Everything else is just reality television from a would-be showman.

January 2019

Wrong Way Corrigan

Governor Stitt appointed former private school administrator Michael Rogers to be his Secretary of State. Then, he named former private school administrator Michael Rogers to be his Secretary of Education. Looks good, doesn't it? Two secretaries for the price of one!

Wait! Did our new governor just eliminate the position of Secretary of Education? Can he do that? How does this square with his plan to make Oklahoma a top-ten education state?

In an interview with *The Claremore Progress*'s Kayleigh Thesenvitz, Stitt complained about wasteful spending in the Departments of Transportation, Education, and Corrections.

"We don't have as high a quality," he said. "So I know there is waste because we're spending the same amount of money as every other state does."

As much money as other states, huh?

According to *Education Week*, in 2018 Oklahoma spent 9,227 dollars per pupil. That's more than 25 percent less than the national average of 12,526 dollars. One of the ways we spend less is to pack more and more students into a single classroom.

To cut waste, Governor Stitt wants a financial audit of every single agency every year at a cost of about 50,000 dollars per agency per year. He must be expecting an awful lot of waste.

And what waste would that be? Textbooks? Technology? Librarians? Those pesky principals?

Is privatization your goal, Governor Stitt? It's worked so well for the Department of Corrections, with guaranteed occupancy rates, record numbers of Oklahoma prisoners, and dangerously low levels of staff.

There's a direct link between education funding and incarceration rates. How much does private profit siphon off money that should be spent in the classroom?

Forty percent of Americans are one missed paycheck away from poverty. These are working people. Will it be their children who benefit if we privatize?

The governor says he can make all this work without raising revenue.

As if that's not enough, Todd Russ's HB2214 would strip teachers of their licenses if they walk out of the classroom. Mark Allen's SB 592 would require a 50,000-dollar bond before any group of more than 100 people could assemble on Capitol grounds.

Senator Allen, does that include more than 100 legislators?

How much will it cost the state to defend an attack on the right to peaceably assemble?

You thought the last eight years were hard on educators and education in Oklahoma! It's a long way from number forty-seven to top ten, especially if we're heading in the wrong direction.

February 2019

Why Are You Afraid?

Why do some people get downright belligerent when you mention the word socialism? They've been programed to get mad about it. They've been conned into being afraid of it. Politicians who can't win on working policies have learned to win with misdirection. Make people afraid of something or someone, and they will vote against their own interests.

Is the situation dire in Venezuela? Yes. Is it because of socialism?

No. It's not socialism if a dictator seizes public companies and keeps them for himself and a few generals. Venezuela isn't a socialist country. It is a lesson in how quickly a thriving democracy can become a dictatorship. This, not some abstract economic theory, is why we should be afraid.

You don't have to hate socialism to love capitalism. Economics isn't either/or, regardless of what you've been taught to oppose. We can start our own businesses, engage in vigorous commerce, and still have a social safety net paid for by reasonable taxes.

Do you hate regulations?

Do you flinch when someone throws out the term government overreach?

How do you feel about unions?

I daresay what you believe about any of these things you believe either because of experience, because you've done your research, or because some politician or talking head convinced you with their talking points. Only two of these reasons are valid.

We will not be free in this country unless people do their own thinking. We will not be free if we are ruled by fear and loathing (to borrow an apt phrase) manufactured to control you.

Engage in conversation, read widely, and think for yourself! But all that won't do any good unless you vote your convictions. Vote in every election. If you don't, you can just sit back and watch our hard-earned freedoms taken away by those who are up to no good.

March 2019

Let's Talk about Guns

It never occurred to me that a shotgun was anything but a necessary tool, on my grandfather's ranch or on my small homestead. While I'm not prepared to give up my .410 when there are water moccasins that stray too far from the creek bank, I've begun to question my own beliefs.

How much firepower is too much for individuals? Who has the right to decide?

Here are a few more questions about gun ownership and gun rights to which I'd like answers.

Is the NRA the largest registry of gun owners in the world?

What can be done with a list like that?

If democracy falls, would listed gun owners that speak out against the person or group in power be targeted?

What is the real purpose of the list? Marketing? Political power? Gun control?

Would it be possible to regulate what manufacturers are allowed to sell to the public?

Yeah, I realize that when corporations are in charge of the political system, that's a stupid question.

What makes some people need to display their firepower?

Is a conceal carry license an unnecessary expense in Oklahoma?

Does a background check for gun ownership curtail freedom any more than a background check for employment?

Can we be truly free if we can't own any weapon we choose?

Can we be truly free if we are afraid to send our children to school?

Which is the greater threat to freedom?

Why can't we sit down and talk about these things without choosing sides? I mean, just bring up the topic of gun rights and both sides are on their knees loading and taking aim.

Yes, I know I'm sometimes guilty. I know that there are a lot of topics in addition to Second Amendment rights to which my question applies.

But, please, can we talk?

April 2019

Wait! You Thought I Was Talking about Venezuela?

Consolidate.
Trim the government to just a few
loyal minions.

Ignore the Constitution.
Create an enemy, and
promise to save us all,
or at least the ones who voted for you.

Profess your base's religion, and
make their issues yours,
despite all the evidence
of your lack of values,
your belief in only one god,
yourself.

It is enough
that they want to believe
that you believe.

Of course, none of this works
if voters trust the press
or the courts
or Congress
or anybody who isn't you,
so cast doubt like penny candy
at a homecoming parade.

And there, you have it,
the ease with which a would-be dictator
takes down a once-thriving democracy.

April 2019

Why We Need Reading Teachers

I'm still trying to wrap my mind around why anyone would vote for a man who filed repeatedly for bankruptcy because "we need a good businessman in the White House." Let's grab a dictionary and look up the definition of bankruptcy.

Do you understand the moral bankruptcy of cheating contractors, of taking your cut off the top and letting investors carry the losses?

A news story this morning said legislators' expenses were going up, so their salaries were being increased. How many of these same legislators have voted against the minimum wage increase? Do you agree with their assessment that raising minimum wage would hurt businesses, but working two jobs and still living below the poverty line is okay for the little guy?

Maybe you don't understand cause and effect. How often do the wealthy amass their fortunes alone, without staff, sales people, and an army of workers? Is it okay for workers to be paid less than what they need to get by? Even Henry Ford understood that his workers should be able to afford one of the cars they built for him and his company.

Comprehension is a skill that's improved by asking questions and thinking things through.

How many of the president's supporters have even read *The Art of the Deal*? Do they still appreciate the deals he's making with China (and Mexico and Canada), deals that are costing American farmers billions? Does it make sense that American taxpayers have to pony up to keep farmers afloat because of the president's deal making? And does it make sense that many farmers still support this deal-making president?

This is not liberal fiscal policy versus conservative fiscal policy, it's about making sense. It doesn't make sense to spend billions to keep the people who are willing to work in our fields and in our houses out. It doesn't make sense to manufacture a crisis at the border by not hiring enough immigration judges to handle the influx. It doesn't make sense to ignore why people are making the dangerous trek to our border.

It doesn't make sense to slap tariffs on goods that increase the cost of those goods, especially if you're not going to raise the minimum wage so workers can pay the increased cost.

Maybe universities aren't hotbeds of liberal thinking at all. Maybe they are hotbeds of comprehension and common sense. Maybe those who think the president is on the right track need to go back to school, or at least start asking questions and thinking things through.

May 2019

Scary Times

The United States has never been kind to all its citizens. The natives of this continent weren't even granted citizenship, the right to vote, to have a say in governance, until the 1920s. Yes, that includes the heroic Choctaw code talkers of World War I.

Slaves were actual property with fewer rights than my dog has now. I can be charged with cruelty to animals, but slave owners had no such constraints. Ownership gave one the right of rape, beatings, and murder, the right to sell a woman's child from her arms.

As part of the privileged (white, landowning) class, I didn't appreciate how fragile a human's rights could be until I got out into the wider world, had a chance to see how other people live. A good many of my fellow citizens haven't had their eyes opened yet. Or perhaps they really do believe the lie that God gave this land to the conquerors.

Conquerors are merely thieves. I can claim that at least my Quaker ancestors purchased their land from the original inhabitants, but I'm not sure they even had the right to do that. What grants us the right to be born and to die, to live where we are or migrate to another place?

Animals have always fought for territory. Bulls have fought for the right to mate. Animals with few or no predators can wipe out native populations.

Humans are animals. We try to claim special status, but right now I'm seeing an especially dangerous breed on the loose in this country, and I'm afraid.

If you aren't afraid of this administration, of the income-inequality-widening policies of the GOP, of nationalism, of the way refugees are treated as something less than human, it is either because you have purposefully made yourself blind, choosing to see what you want to see, or you are choosing to not look at all.

When people are struggling day to day just to survive, they have little time for philosophy and politics. They see no meaning in their vote. But educating ourselves and voting is the only sane weapon we have right now.

How do we get out the vote? How do we educate people to vote in their own best interest? What can we do to save this country, to be as high-minded as we like to tell ourselves we are?

June 2019

Most Dangerous Man, Part 1

The most dangerous man in America thinks being gay is a choice. He believes the high rate of suicide among young gay people is because they are fighting nature and are in torment.

Doesn't sound like much of a choice, does it?

He and others like him pile on the torment, telling them they're going to hell. Conversion therapy and convincing them they are sinners is how they'll save their souls. And if that doesn't work, they kick them out of their churches, some even out of their homes.

That seems like an extreme way to help someone change his or her mind.

This dangerous man thinks Sodom and Gomorrah were destroyed because of sodomy.

I read that story. If it's about sodomy, why doesn't it say? It's a leap to say that the righteous man in this morality tale means heterosexual man. Burning the city is a radical way to deal with the lack of righteousness or homosexuality.

What about the righteous women? It leaves us in doubt about Lot's wife. Why was she looking back? Did she know what was in store for her daughters, you know, the ones who bear their own half siblings because they've been taught that not having children is a greater sin than incest?

The dangerous man thinks abortion is murder. Every fertilized egg implanted in a woman's womb must be born.

Rape? Maybe it was her fault. She shouldn't have gotten drunk.

There are no Bible verses to protect a pregnant eleven-year-old from incest or rape, just a dangerous man saying, "Keep sexuality out of the classroom. Let kids be kids."

Except when they get pregnant?

The dangerous man doesn't believe in sex education. He wants to see Planned Parenthood shut down. He believes cities are filled with "girlymen and metrosexuals."

What is a metrosexual, anyway? A man who reads, perhaps? A man who thinks his partner is a whole person and not just a vessel? A man who believes women can make their own reproductive choices?

He's one man, you say. Yes, one man, but he's part of an army in this country, men who believe in the patriarchy. Women, too.

June 2019

Most Dangerous Man, Part 2

The most dangerous man in America believes in the Bible. This is not what makes him dangerous.

What makes him dangerous is his disdain for anyone who doesn't believe the way he does.

His God is a loving God who is going to save him. If you don't get saved from tornadoes, floods, and wildfires, either you are a sinner or God has a good reason.

He doesn't believe in climate change. The idea that humans can destroy the world is a plot cooked up by that old socialist Al Gore. Whole neighborhoods along the coasts are losing ground to rising water. Island nations in the Pacific are disappearing.

Not our fault, he says.
Let's drill in the Arctic, he says.
Let's build a wall.

Wars, income inequality, and the climate change in which he doesn't believe have ramped up migration around the world. He doesn't want immigrants here.

Not all dangerous men are white, but this one is. He claims he isn't a racist, but he's worried about all the brown people asking for asylum. Criminals, he calls them.

He doesn't agree that asking for asylum is legal, but he has no regard for facts.

Or scale. He says all politicians lie. He doesn't see the difference between one lie and 6,000.

He believes we are a country of laws, but the president is above the law.

He believes the forty-fourth president destroyed America's standing in the world and the forty-fifth president is restoring it.

There's more irony here than I can process.

He's afraid that noncitizens will vote.

He's afraid that minorities and poor people will vote the wrong way, and he's willing to change the laws to make voting harder. We are a country of laws, you know.

He's afraid of losing status, of losing power, of everything but this cruel administration.

He's one man, one of many. And you can bet that he and his climate-change-denying, immigrant-fearing army vote.

July 2019

I Can't Hear You!

There's a lot of disinformation available if you want to fool yourself into believing that everything is okay. Given my anxiety level these days, I'm tempted to turn off social media and the news and fantasize about the world I want, a world in which the president and his administration care about humanity and believe in the Constitution.

Turning off is not an option, though. We can't surrender. We can't be quiet.

Apathy is our enemy. So is silence. If I may revise an old saying: action and truth will set us free.

When the president is the Liar-in-Chief, you must be especially vigilant. When he lies, make sure you have your own facts straight, and speak up. As my friend, Claudia, says, do it again and again.

Will everyone listen? No. Will someone listen? Maybe, and that's why we have to keep setting the record straight.

Let's start with a few facts about immigration:

1) It was Jeff Sessions who initiated President Trump's Family Separation Policy.
2) It is legal to ask for asylum.
3) When you ask for asylum, it is the duty of our government to have immigration judges in place to hear your case.
4) Children who experience trauma in their lives are permanently affected. Humane people don't inflect such trauma.
5) U.S. foreign policy, official and unofficial, legal and illegal, contributes to the mess that compels citizens in Guatemala, Honduras, and El Salvador to flee their homes.
6) President Obama deported many undocumented visitors.
7) President Obama signed the Dream Act because Congress refused to act.
8) One more time, President Trump must take full responsibility for Family Separation as a policy to deter immigration.
9) Family separation, as a deterrent, did not work.

It's an act of patriotism to counter lies with truth. Speak up while we still can.

About the Author

Sharon Edge Martin is a reading specialist and writer whose stories and poems have appeared in dozens of publications, including *Alfred Hitchcock Mystery Magazine, Oklahoma Today, Outside,* Michael Bugeja's *The Art and Craft of Poetry*, and in three Woody Guthrie anthologies. She is a regular contributor to *The Oklahoma Observer* and the host of a monthly poetry reading at Tidewater Winery in Drumright, Oklahoma.

Martin is the author of *Froggy Bottom Blues*, a picture book, and *Not a Prodigal*, a poetry collection that was a finalist for the Oklahoma Book Award in 2019.

She lives in rural Oklahoma with her husband, artist Dale Martin.

About the Cover Artist

Dale Martin has been designated a Master Pastelist by the Pastel Society of America. His paintings are in private and corporate collections, including those of General Motors, IBM, Northwestern University, Oklahoma Natural Gas, State of New Mexico Art in Public Places Project, and in the Phippen Museum of Western Art in Prescott, Arizona.

His paintings have been included in *Pure Color: The Best of Pastel, 200 Great Painting Ideas for Artists, Southwest Art, Oklahoma Today,* and on the covers of *Pastel Journal* and *Sedona Monthly*. He also illustrated *Not a Prodigal*, a poetry collection by his wife, Sharon Edge Martin.

Voting is a solemn choice.

**Not voting is also a choice,
a reckless one.**

CPSIA information can be obtained
at www.ICGtesting.com
Printed in the USA
BVHW051913060320
574292BV00004B/16